The Wallowa Mountains

A Natural History Guide

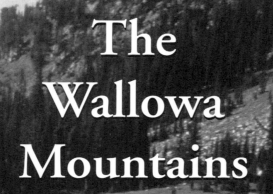

The Wallowa Mountains

A Natural History Guide

Keith Pohs

Northwest MountainWorks

Cover Photographs

Background, forest along Eagle Creek in early fall.
Front inset top, Mirror Lake and Eagle Cap.
Front inset middle, forest of ponderosa pine in winter.
Front inset bottom, peak above South Fork Imnaha River.
Back inset top, the Matterhorn from near Ice Lake.
Back inset bottom, Glacier Lake and Glacier Peak at sunrise.

All photographs by the author.
Book design by Keith Pohs.
Book layout by Eben Rose.

Line drawings of birds and animals are by Lisa Hall and Ellen Blonder and are courtesy of the California Wildlife Habitat Relationships Program (from Zeiner, et al.
1989-1991). Line drawings of trees are from a reprint by Dover Publications of an
original manual published by the United States Forest Service in 1908, George B.
Sudworth's Forest Trees of the Pacific Slope. Line drawings of grasses are from
Common Plants of the Inland Pacific Northwest, by Charles Grier Johnson, Jr.,
USFS Pacific Northwest Region Publication R6-NR-ECOL-TP-04-98, and are
courtesy of the University of Washington Press as originally published in "Vascular
Plants of the Pacific Northwest" by Hitchcock, et al., 1977.

For author correspondence and ordering information please visit:
        www.wallowaguide.com
on the Internet or write
        Wallowa Guide, Northwest MountainWorks,
        P.O. Box 91313, Portland, OR 97291.

The author takes full responsibility for all errors and omissions.

ISBN 0-9679138-0-2
Library of Congress Card Number 00-101172

ACKNOWLEDGMENTS

I would first like to thank all of the research scientists who have worked in the Wallowa Mountains and the entire Blue Mountain region. Their studies form the basis of this guidebook. Without the work of these and untold others this book would simply not have been possible.

I'd like to thank a number of people for reviewing the manuscript in its various stages. Jane Rohling of the United States Forest Service's Wallowa Mountains Visitor Center in Enterprise was a great help, both providing me with valuable information and carefully reviewing the document several times, even in its early rudimentary form. Bob Carson, Professor of Geology and Environmental Studies at Whitman College, generously reviewed the manuscript and offered helpful suggestions and comments. Thanks for your time and inspiration both at Whitman and during the writing of this work. Author Chris Maser, Mary Swanson of The Bookloft, and Frank Conley of Eagle Cap Fishing Guides also reviewed the entire manuscript, courtesy of Oregon State University Press, and Patrick Matthews of the Oregon Department of Fish and Wildlife reviewed the fauna section early on. My good friend Stephen Kalberer and Katherine Berg also reviewed the manuscript in its entirety. Thank you.

Warren Slesinger of Oregon State University Press offered guidance and constructive ideas that helped greatly improve the manuscript. Thank you for your interest and support.

Eben Rose did the final layout and Mark Middleton of Four Seasons Color did much of the imaging for the book. Kim Hallum and Cindy Soqui at Northland Graphics did numerous late stage changes to get the book to press. Thank you all for your patience and excellent work.

I would like to thank J. Dale Nations, my advisor in the Earth Science program at Northern Arizona University, and Michael Kelly and James Wittke for allowing me the freedom to undertake this project and for their patience. Several employees of the Center for Environmental Sciences and Education at Northern Arizona University helped me in numerous ways, including Sally Evans, Tom Sisk, Mike Kelly, Michael Ort, Carol Haden, R. Scott Anderson, Paul Rowland, Constance Benally, Nicolette Cooley, and John Grahame. Jim Maxka and Charlie Kaetz were helpful in dealing with computer matters.

I want to thank a few friends and family for supporting me throughout this project and over the years. Stephen Kalberer and Andy Hager have accompanied me on many trips into the range over the last decade, and Aaron Merrill has always offered positive and enthusiastic energy. Kimberly Coyle has been a true godsend in my life. My sister Kathy, my brother Ken, and my sister Karen have always been supportive, and Karen in particular was a help and inspiration throughout the writing of this work. My mother and father, Arlene and Ray, have supported me, perhaps hesitantly in a few cases, in all my endeavors since I can remember, and without whom this book would not have been possible. Thank you!

For My Family

CONTENTS

INTRODUCTION

The Wallowa Mountains are among the most spectacular in the state of Oregon. Rising more than a vertical mile above the sagebrush plains and grasslands of the northeastern corner of the state, the mountains form an impressive skyline of snow and rock visible to all who live in or visit this quiet region. The range's alpine core, the High Wallowas, is a dramatic landscape of sharp peaks, lake-filled basins, rich coniferous forests, and deep, glacially carved valleys. In contrast, many of the Wallowas' lowermost flanks form a scenic mosaic of grassy slopes, rolling forested ridges, and rugged, narrow river canyons. Today much of the Wallowa country is public land, some of which is preserved within the Eagle Cap Wilderness, Oregon's largest and perhaps finest designated wilderness area. And though certain parts of the Wallowa high country are increasingly popular with visitors, solitude can still be found for those willing to explore the more isolated areas of the range.

The natural history of the Wallowa Mountains is as interesting as the area's exceptionally scenic landscape. The range is notable for its diversity of flora and fauna, a reflection of the mountains' geographic location and topography, as well as its varied geologic history. The Wallowas are somewhat of a crossroads for plant and animal species inhabiting two distinctly different geographic regions: the maritime Cascade region of western Oregon and Washington and the continental Rocky Mountain areas of western Idaho and Montana. The climate of this corner of Oregon is much different from that found nearer the Pacific Ocean. The higher and drier terrain of the Wallowa Mountains and the surrounding area supports a different mix of vegetation and wildlife than is commonly found in the generally wetter and much milder climate of western Oregon. Though several species of coastal origin also inhabit the area, species more common to the inland ranges of the Rocky Mountains make up a significant portion of the region's flora and fauna. There are also elements of Great Basin flora and fauna in the range, particularly to the south, making the Wallowas a link between several major ecosystem types found in the western United States. In addition to this biotic diversity, the area's geologic evolution differs greatly from that of most of western Oregon, where volcanoes of the Coast and Cascade Ranges dominate the landscape. This varied geologic history, combined with an intermediate position between two different climatic regimes, has led to an assemblage of rocks, plants, and animals unique to the area.

Geography

Considered a subrange of the Blue Mountains complex of central and eastern Oregon and southeastern Washington, the Wallowa Mountains are easily the largest and the highest of the ranges comprising the "Blues"(Figure 1). Other mountain ranges of the Blues include the Ochoco, Aldrich, Strawberry, Greenhorn, and Elkhorn Mountains, as well as the Blue Mountains proper, a broad, dissected plateau stretching from southwest of Pendleton northeastward to the Wenaha-Tucannon country along the Oregon-Washington border. Geographically these areas comprise the forested highlands of the state east of the Cascades and north of the fault-block ranges of the Great Basin, such as Steens Mountain and Hart Mountain in southeastern Oregon. The extensive inland forests that cover thousands of acres in the Blue Mountain ranges are predominantly publicly owned. The

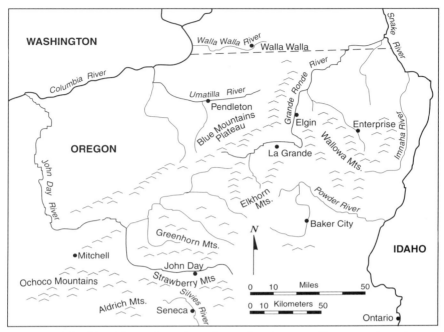

Figure 1. The Blue Mountain region of central and eastern Oregon and southeastern Washington. The Wallowa Mountains are at the eastern edge of the region in northeastern Oregon.

United States Forest Service manages much of the acreage in four separate national forests: the Ochoco, Malheur, Umatilla, and Wallowa-Whitman National Forests.

From the air, the Wallowa Mountains appear as a slightly oblong dome of high peaks trending roughly northwest-southeast. The range becomes progressively higher and more alpine as one travels along its length from west to east, culminating in the area surrounding the Lakes Basin and the divides just to the north. The Powder River valley lies to the south and southwest of the mountains, the Grande Ronde River valley to the west and northwest, and the Joseph uplands and beautiful Wallowa River valley to the north. The mountains' eastern slope merges with a mid-elevation plateau overlooking the awesome gorge of Hells Canyon and across the Snake River the Seven Devils Mountains of Idaho.

Figure 2. One of the many spectacular valleys of the High Wallowas. Here Eagle Cap rises above the cold, clear waters of East Eagle Creek.

The Eagle Cap Wilderness

The Wallowa Mountains' scenic and recreational value was first recognized legally in 1930, when 220,000 acres of the range were set aside as a primitive area by the United States Forest Service. This original primitive area, one of the first in Oregon, was classified as wilderness in 1940. Named after the prominent dome of Eagle Cap, the Eagle Cap Wilderness became a part of the National Wilderness Preservation System with the passage of the Wilderness Act in 1964. Since that time the wilderness has twice been expanded to include more of the area's spectacular landscape. In 1972 73,000 acres were added, followed by another 65,000 acres with the passage of the Oregon Wilderness Bill in 1984. The 1984 bill added a significant portion of lower-elevation acreage (rare in most wilderness bills because these lands are commonly valuable for timber or agriculture), including stands of ponderosa pine along and near the Minam River in the northwestern section of the wilderness. The Eagle Cap Wilderness is the largest in the state of Oregon, covering over 360,000 acres (560 square miles) of rugged mountainous country.

Despite the great distance of this area from major metropolitan centers, parts of the Eagle Cap Wilderness are heavily used by hikers, horseback riders, hunters, backcountry skiers, and even a few mountaineers. Elevations within the wilderness range from 3000 feet in the lower Minam River valley to over 9800 feet atop both Sacajawea and the Matterhorn, a difference of nearly 7000 feet. This great contrast in elevation allows the wilderness traveler to observe many distinct ecological zones while hiking along the trails that traverse the mountains. The local climate, topography, vegetation, and wildlife change noticeably as one climbs from the lowest river valleys and grasslands, through the montane and subalpine forests, and finally to the bare rock and alpine tundra of the highest peaks.

Lakes

Commonly surrounded by lush meadows, picturesque groves of fir and pine, and large slabs of glacially scoured bedrock, the many scenic subalpine lakes of the High Wallowas are popular destinations for those visiting the high country. Most of these lakes occupy basins between 7000 and 8000 feet in elevation, and most have formed in areas underlain by granitic bedrock. Snow does not melt off some of these high basins until mid-summer, when the ice cover of the lakes finally breaks up. Glacier, Prospect, Razz and Billy Jones Lakes are all well above 8000 feet in elevation and may be partially ice-covered until the end of July in cooler, wetter years. Legore Lake, tucked away at 8972 feet in a treeless basin in the northern part of the range, is one of the highest lakes in the state, and is the highest in Oregon to sustain a viable population of fish (introduced trout). Of the fifty or so named lakes found in the backcountry, Mirror, Glacier, Ice, Minam, Chimney, and Aneroid Lakes are some of the most visited.

Figure 3. Glacier Peak rises dramatically above Glacier Lake.

The most popular and famous lake of the Wallowa Mountains is only partly in the range, extending out past the mountain front into the Wallowa valley. Situated below the northeast side of Chief Joseph Mountain, Wallowa Lake extends over three miles from its northern shore to its southern end below Mt. Bonneville. Damming the lake and flanking its sides all the way to the mountain front are spectacular glacial moraines. These grassy ridges, formed by an ancient glacier, rise nearly 1000 feet above the lake. A popular state park, complete with large cottonwoods and picnic tables, lies at the southern shore of the lake.

Rivers and Creeks

The major rivers and tributary creeks draining the High Wallowas form a pronounced radial drainage pattern centered around Eagle Cap and the Lakes Basin (Figure 4). The Lakes Basin is an

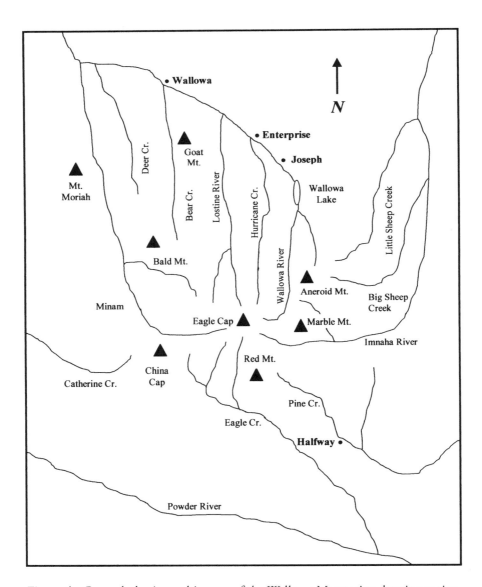

Figure 4. General physiographic map of the Wallowa Mountains showing major drainages and selected peaks. The principal rivers and creeks of the Wallowas form a pronounced radial drainage pattern around Eagle Cap and the Lakes Basin area.

exceptionally scenic, lightly forested subalpine plateau nestled beneath the north face of Eagle Cap in the central Wallowas. Many of the trails in the range lead directly to this popular lake-dotted region. The principle waterways of the range radiate out in every direction from this area: Eagle Creek flowing to the south, the Minam River to the west, the Lostine River, Hurricane Creek, and the Wallowa River to the north, and the Imnaha River flowing out the eastern end of the range toward the Snake River. Catherine Creek, Deer Creek, Bear Creek, and Big and Little Sheep Creeks are other major creeks draining the high slopes of the range. The steep valley walls above these rushing rivers and creeks are commonly 2000 to 3000 feet high, in some areas over 4000 feet high, and in the narrower drainages avalanche-scarred ridges soaring above small meadows make for spectacular views while traveling along the lower trails. Portions of some of the ranges' waterways, including stretches of the Lostine, Minam, and Imnaha Rivers and Eagle Creek, have been designated National Wild and Scenic Rivers for their exceptional beauty.

The principal rivers and creeks of the mountains characteristically tumble swiftly through large boulders and over small waterfalls on their way out of the mountains to the basins below. Near their headwaters in the interior of the range, many can show a different character, meandering through large meadows in quiet riffles and deep pools. Further downvalley, smaller tributary streams cascade down the steep valley sides of the major drainages, occasionally hopping tens of feet or more from cliffs to form waterfalls. Some of these, spiraling downslope in a loud torrent of white foam and rushing water, have cut spectacular, narrow gorges through hard bedrock. Adam Creek is an excellent example, roaring 2300 feet down from its origin at Ice Lake, over a large waterfall, and through a tight, winding canyon before dumping into the West Fork of the Wallowa River.

Above Timberline

Many veteran Cascade Range backpackers and mountaineers are surprised to learn that the Wallowa Mountains contain the largest

Figure 5. Bear Creek in the northwestern Wallowas.

continuous area of subalpine and alpine terrain in Oregon. The high-est peak, according to the most recent surveys, is Sacajawea, whose massive marble faces rise above Hurricane Creek to a height of 9838 feet. Just to the south, the equally impressive Matterhorn, until recently considered the highest point in the Wallowas, rises above the frigid waters of Ice Lake to a slightly lower elevation of 9826 feet.

These two are the sixth and seventh highest mountains in Oregon, surpassed in height by Mount Hood, Mount Jefferson, and the Three Sisters of the Cascade Range, all of which top 10,000 feet.

Earlier trail and topographic maps listed the Matterhorn at 10,004 feet, then 9845 feet, but the elevation has since been changed to the 9826-foot figure as it appears on a recent map of the area. Red Mountain, at the southern edge of the wilderness, rises to 9555 feet, while Eagle Cap's graceful granitic profile, at 9572 feet, overlooks much of the central portion of the range. The eastern Wallowas are dominated by the brown dome of Aneroid Mountain in the north at 9702 feet and Marble Mountain in the south, which rises swiftly to nearly 9000 feet above the South Fork of the Imnaha River. Some of the higher peaks in the western part of the range include High Hat Butte, at 8160 feet, and the 8000-foot high ridge of Goat Mountain. The higher peaks often occur along interconnected crests and long ridgelines. Thus one main ridge may have a number of prominent "peaks" along its length, as in the case of the divide separating the East and West Forks of the Wallowa River. Petes Point, Sentinel Peak, and Cusick Mountain all rise above 9000 feet along this divide.

Summits of major peaks in the High Wallowas are commonly thousands of feet above adjacent valley floors. Krag Peak, at the southern entrance to the spectacular upper canyon of the East Fork of Eagle Creek, rises 4400 feet in a horizontal distance of just over one and a half miles from the valley floor at 4600 feet to its summit just over 9000 feet. This is a gradient of nearly 3000 feet per mile. The huge wall of the Matterhorn rises 3100 feet above the Hurricane Creek valley in less than a mile, the final 1800 feet up the nearly vertical west face. Katy Mountain and a point above Cheval Lake, both overlooking the upper Minam River valley, rise 3000 feet in just over a mile. Average relief in the range, the difference in elevation between immediately adjacent high and low areas, is approximately 3000 feet. Peering over the edge of these steep-sided peaks thousands of feet down into the many gaping, glacially scoured valleys of the range is one of the more exhilarating experiences one can have while hiking or climbing among these mountains.

Figure 6. Eagle Cap, Glacier Peak, and the Lakes Basin from near the summit of the Matterhorn.

Despite this topographic relief and some areas of excellent rock, the Wallowas have only a few walls of interest to climbers. All peaks have walk-up sides and climbing opportunities are generally limited. The sheer 1800-foot west face of the Matterhorn is an exception, and a few other faces in the range may offer short technical routes for interested mountaineers.

CLIMATE

The climate of the Wallowa Mountains and the surrounding region may be considered a mix of that of the northern Rocky Mountains to the east and the Cascade Range to the west. In general, the range is sunnier, drier, and colder than the Cascades, where a mild maritime climate prevails, but it is also wetter than the other ranges of the Blue Mountains and most ranges to the east. Despite the mountains' inland position, and the subsequent rainshadow effect of the coastal ranges of western Oregon, parts of the Wallowas manage to wring out more than 70 inches of precipitation a year, easily making this the wettest area in the state east of the Cascade Range.

As storm clouds approach the mountains from the west they are forced to rise, cool, and drop much of their moisture. This process, known as **orographic** lifting, results in increased precipitation at higher elevations (Figure 7). The broad Wallowa uplift effectively forces moisture from passing storm clouds, resulting in fairly high precipitation for the range's height and geographic position. The crest of the much narrower Elkhorn Mountains, just to the west, is nearly as high as the Wallowa crest, yet this range receives only about 40 inches of precipitation a year. The result of the Wallowa's abundant precipitation is a lusher mountain landscape than is typically found in other Blue Mountain ranges, where

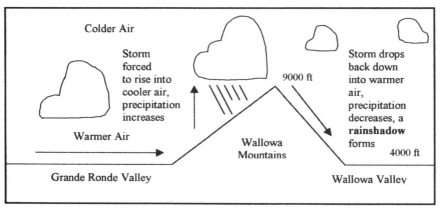

Figure 7. The process of orographic lifting and the rainshadow effect greatly influence the local climate of the Wallowa region. As storms commonly approach the region from the west or southwest, they are forced to rise up and over the Wallowa crest, resulting in heavier precipitation at higher elevations in the mountains. On the lee side of the range to the east and northeast, a rainshadow forms over the towns of Enterprise and Joseph in the Wallowa Valley.

annual precipitation does not often exceed 50 inches, and is more commonly 30 to 40 inches a year.

As the Cascade Range casts a **rainshadow** over all of eastern Oregon, the high crest of the Wallowas produces a smaller, more local rainshadow over areas to the north and east of the range. As cool air passing over the mountains from the southwest descends down into the Wallowa Valley, the air's ability to hold moisture correspondingly increases with the rise in temperature. As a result, precipitation drastically diminishes to the northeast and east of the range (the lee side of the range) as most storms approach from the west and southwest (the windward side). This rainshadow effect is quite apparent when looking at precipitation data for towns in the Wallowa Valley. The town of Enterprise receives just 16" of precipitation a year, while the summit of Chief Joseph Mountain, only a few miles to the south but more importantly over 5000 feet higher, likely receives more than 50" a year. The town of Wallowa receives more precipitation than Joseph, about 20 miles to the east, despite being approximately 1000 feet lower. Joseph lies directly below some of the highest peaks in the range, which form a more pronounced rainshadow than the lower northwestern range near Wallowa. Most precipitation in the mountains occurs as snow, while periodic rainstorms in the fall and late spring and occasional summer thunderstorms during the summer account for the rest of the Wallowas' precipitation.

Most people visit the range during the summer months, especially July and August when much of the high country is free of snow. Typical for the Northwest, this is the hottest and driest time of the year. Early June can be quite cool and some of the last snows of the season may fall on the higher terrain (though it can snow any time of the year at the higher elevations). By the end of June, summer has taken hold of most areas, with daytime highs in the valleys usually in the 70s or 80s. Thunderstorms, accompanied by strong winds and lightning, may occur periodically throughout the summer months. These storms occasionally result in significant precipitation, but usually bring only a brief shower. Most of August is characteristically clear and quite warm but by the end of the month hints of autumn appear, as nights become cooler and some high plants can begin to change color following the earliest frosts.

Autumn is an excellent time to visit the range. Days are commonly sunny and mild while nights are clear and frosty. Mid-September high temperatures in the higher basins are generally in the 50s or low 60s but by the end of the month highs in the 40s are increasingly common. Early October generally brings crisp, clear weather as well as the beautiful color change of the western larch and other deciduous trees. The predominantly fair weather of "Indian summer" is periodically interrupted by brief snowstorms, adding a light dusting of snow to the peaks. These storms usually do not last very long, perhaps a full day, and the snow often quickly melts off many areas as sunny skies return. The first major snowfall of the year in the range can occur as early as September but more commonly occurs in middle or late October.

November usually marks the beginning of deep winter for most of the high country, as snowstorms pass with some regularity,

Figure 8. Red Mountain from Hawkins Pass in mid-July of a particularly cool and wet year.

blanketing the peaks in fresh snow. Over the next several weeks the snowline descends, often reaching the valley floors by the end of November or early December. Strong low-pressure systems, many of which originate in the Gulf of Alaska, make their way towards the Pacific coastal states and eventually across the interior basins to the ranges of the Blue Mountains. Some colder, larger storms can drop 2 to 3 feet of snow above 7000 feet, with six inches to perhaps a foot accumulating on the valley floors. In contrast, most winters also have long periods of fair weather when large high-pressure systems shield the Northwest from these Pacific storms. During these periods of stable weather, which usually occur in January or February, clear skies can prevail for a week or more. Temperature inversions are common at this time, as the denser, colder air of the mountains filters down into the valleys at night. The stagnant nature of the air mass prevents recirculation of this colder air, leading to a **temperature inversion**. The valley floors remain quite cold, often in a blanket of fog, while the higher peaks bask in relatively warm sunshine. March is the snowiest month of the year in the region. By this time in late winter the jet stream is often firmly planted across the Pacific Northwest and a succession of storms lined up in the eastern Pacific continually flow across the area.

Spring comes late to this part of Oregon. The leaves of the many deciduous trees in the lower valleys do not appear until late April or May. Some areas, such as the lower Minam River valley, may be clear of snow in April and over the course of the next few months the snowline slowly recedes back up to the higher reaches of the range. Areas above 7000 feet are usually snow-covered until the middle of July. The north-facing sides of the higher passes, such as Hawkins or Horton passes, are usually not free of snow until August. The wildflower meadows of the range usually peak around mid-July.

Climatological records for the Wallowa Mountains are scarce, but records for towns in the surrounding valleys combined with some information from automated stations high up in the range give a general picture of the climate in this part of Oregon. The inland position of the region and the fairly high elevations result in great daily and seasonal temperature fluctuations. Table 1 shows climatic data for towns scattered around the Wallowa Mountains in the Powder, Pine, Grande Ronde, and Wallowa valleys.

Table 1. Temperature Data for Towns of the Wallowa Region.

Town	Elev (ft)	January (°F)	July (°F)	Ext H/L (°F)	Mean T (°F)	Min 32 (°F)
Enterprise	3756	33/13	77/41	96/-33	41	228 days
Baker City	3441	33/16	84/48	106/-39	46	183 days
Union	2792	36/23	84/49	108/-27	48	140 days
Halfway	2621	33/14	88/47	108/-33	46	189 days
LaGrande	2788	38/24	85/53	104/-18	49	136 days

Elev (ft) is the elevation in feet of the recording station. **January** and **July** columns are average daily high and low temperatures. Extreme high and extreme low (Ext H/L) are all-time records. **Mean T** is the average temperature for the entire year. **Min 32** column is average number of days per year the daily low is below 32 degrees. (Data courtesy of the Oregon Climate Service.)

Enterprise, in the Wallowa River valley, is the coolest area near the range, with lows dropping below freezing 228 days a year and a mean annual temperature of only 41 degrees. Nearly half of the days in December and January the high does not reach 32 degrees. The all-time record highs and lows for the above stations are consistent with many areas of the intermountain West where temperatures can fluctuate tremendously both seasonally and daily. The records for the town of Baker City, in the Powder River Valley, span a temperature range of 146 degrees! Table 2 gives various precipitation data for the same recording stations.

Table 2. Precipitation Data for Towns of the Wallowa Region.

Town	Elev (ft)	An ppt (in)	An snf (in)	snf/ppt	wet mth	dry mth
Enterprise	3756	16	49	3.1	May	Oct
Baker City	3441	10	26	2.6	May	July
Union	2792	14	24	1.7	May	July
Halfway	2621	22	69	3.1	Jan	July
LaGrande	2788	17	26	1.5	Nov	July

Elev (ft) is the elevation in feet of the recording station. An ppt and An snf columns are annual precipitation and snowfall in inches. Snf/ppt is a ratio of how much of the annual precipitation is snowfall (the higher the number, the greater the percentage of annual ppt falls as snow). Wet mth and dry mth are the wettest and driest months of the year. (Data courtesy of the Oregon Climate Service.)

Table 2 shows Halfway, located in the Pine Valley at the southern margin of the range, to be the wettest and snowiest town near the Wallowas, despite the fact that at 2600 feet it is the lowest of the listed recording stations. This area easily receives the most snowfall of any of the stations, and Halfway has recorded annual snow totals exceeding 120 inches twice in both 1975 and 1984. Halfway does not lie in the rainshadow of the High Wallowas, and thus apparently receives more precipitation despite its lower elevation. Its location probably results in the area catching more precipitation from storms approaching from the south and southwest.

Additional climatological information gleaned from more obscure sources for sites nearer the range indicates Sparta (years of record 1891-1926), at 4150 feet, receives roughly 21 inches of annual precipitation, 123 inches of annual snowfall, and has an average temperature of 45.2 degrees. The average date of the last killing frost in spring is May 8, and the average date of the first killing frost in fall is October 14. Sparta has a growing season of approximately 159 days. Cornucopia (28 years of record between 1909 and 1952), a small mining area at 4400 feet just north of Halfway in the Pine Valley, has an average annual precipitation of 44 inches and an average annual snowfall of 280 inches with a maximum of 84 inches occurring in January. This southern end of the range is surprisingly wet.

May is the wettest month for most of the region, with frequent rainstorms passing through the area. July is the driest month of the year for all of the listed stations except Enterprise. This may be due to occasional thunderstorms developing over the high peaks and drifting to the north over the Wallowa Valley, sometimes dropping significant precipitation in just a few minutes. December and January are the snowiest months for the small towns surrounding the Wallowas.

My first trips into the High Wallowas took me to areas readily accessible from the Wallowa Valley, as the north side of the range was easier to reach and many of the most spectacular areas are near Eagle Cap and the divides to the north. On one particular trip, in the middle of August, a friend Andy and I decided to hike up the East Fork Lostine River valley, through the Lakes Basin, and camp at Glacier Lake for a few days. The gorgeous upper Lostine valley is a long, open meadow walled in by granitic slopes on either side. Here the river meanders among lush grasses and scattered fir and pine, with the snow-capped dome of Eagle Cap rising at the head of the valley into, most often in my experience, a deep blue sky.

On this late summer visit, however, heading out from the trailhead, about all we could see were gray clouds overhead, the grass and rocks beneath our feet, and the ghostly forms of dark conifers occasionally piercing a misty blanket of thick fog. Trudging along through the forest, we eventually hit the large meadow of the upper valley, where the winds picked up, and soon we heard a sound familiar to most Northwest hikers, rain pattering on our jackets. Halfway up the meadow we stopped for a quick fuel-up, huddling beneath a grove of dense firs and watching low clouds sweeping across the valley, before we pushed forward to Mirror Lake, where we were greeted by occasional driving sleet and ripping winds. As long as one can easily retreat to a dry tent and fire, I have found that this type of weather can be slightly invigorating, reminding one that

◄——— **Figure 9.** Looking out over Little Frazier Lake toward Pete's Point and Polaris Pass from spectacular Hawkins Pass. The distant peaks are composed of folded strata of the Martin Bridge and Hurwal Formations, while the rocks along the shore of Little Frazier Lake are granodiorite of the Wallowa Batholith.

this landscape is a result of not only sunny days but, more often than not at these elevations, stormy ones such as this late-summer day.

Still focused on reaching Glacier Lake, we wandered through the Lakes Basin and made our way up the switchbacks towards Glacier Pass. At this point we finally decided we needed to set up camp. Our rainwear was soaked, and we were getting chilled to the bone. We climbed up to Glacier Pass, and assuming that the storm couldn't last too long we decided to camp right on the high ridge which separates the lakes below Eagle Cap from the cirque of Glacier Lake.

Waking up the next day I unzipped the rainfly and took a glimpse out of the tent, only to see a dismal view of wispy snowflakes accompanied by gusty winds. Waiting for that summer sun to eventually pierce through the clouds, or at the very least a reasonable let-up in the storm, the next 23 out of 24 hours were spent in the tent, perched on the side of Eagle Cap, enduring a windy, cloudy, rainy, and snowy early-season storm. During those moments stuffed in the tent, I managed to endure several losses in chess, compliments of Andy, as we discussed topics ranging from the contents of our snack bars to the meaning of human existence.

Finally, on Sunday morning, the clouds lifted, and we could see down to Glacier Lake and all the way across to the peaks and ridges of the upper West Fork Wallowa River valley. Although it was still cloudy, the clouds were just grazing the highest crests, and we anxiously decided to get out and head towards Hawkins Pass, where we could get a good view of the Imnaha drainage, which neither of us had seen before. At Hawkins Pass, perhaps the most spectacular in the range, the view before us took in classic Wallowa scenery: Frazier Lake below, complete with floating "snowbergs" and tucked into a deep shadowy cirque beneath the marble walls of Cusick Mountain, across the way, a series of waterfalls cascading down to the valley floor from the high cirque we had just traversed, extending out to the north, the long, U-shaped cleft of the West Fork Wallowa River canyon, and to the south, our first glimpse of the rich green South Fork Imnaha River drainage. The mountains were exhilarating, especially after the seemingly endless time we spent huddled in the tent the day before. The rain and wet snow had freshened the landscape, and the view from the pass out across the dramatic glacially scoured mountains, with the rushing sound of water, the cool damp air sweetened by the storm, and a slight but steady breeze, made this a truly memorable day high in the Wallowas.

Direct snowfall data for the Wallowas is limited, as there are no year-round weather stations in the higher parts of the range other than automated Snowtel sites. Seasonal snowpack is measured periodically in the winter and spring manually, as many irrigators living in the valleys below the range depend on water from the mountains for their crops, but these snowpack measurements do not actually reveal how much snowfall in inches it took to produce what is measured on the ground. The automated stations in the range do record annual precipitation, but they measure purely water equivalent, not actual snowfall depths. Annual precipitation in the heart of the range near Eagle Cap and along the higher divides west of the Lakes Basin is estimated to be over 70 inches, most of it occurring as snow from October through May. Areas farther west are lower in elevation, resulting in less precipitation (estimated 40-60 inches a year). The eastern edge of the range, though much higher than the western Wallowas, also receives less precipitation than the Eagle Cap region as it is in the rainshadow of the central range. The area around Eagle Cap is one of the higher areas in the range, and this combined with the probable funneling effect of the south and west-facing Minam and Eagle Creek river valleys may explain the high precipitation amounts in this region. Many of the highest peaks in the Wallowas (above 9,000 feet) may receive 400 inches of snow a year, while most of the range, from about 6,000 to 8,000 feet, probably averages from 200 to 300 inches of annual snowfall. Regions between 5000 and 6000 feet receive from 100 to 200 inches annually. However, these estimates vary considerably with location. A ridge crest on the western side of the range at 7,000 feet, receiving the brunt of rejuvenated storms passing over lower areas to the west, might have the same annual snowfall as a peak 9,000 feet high on the far eastern slope. Assuming a water equivalent of 10 inches of snow = 1 inch of rain, and that 2/3 of the annual precipitation falls as snow in the higher parts of the range, areas of 60 inches of ppt/yr would receive 400 inches of annual snowfall and areas of 40 inches of ppt/yr would receive 270 inches of snow a year.

GEOLOGY

The geologic diversity of the Wallowa Mountains is truly exceptional, and for their areal extent the Wallowas may be considered one of the most geologically diverse mountain ranges in the country. Many different rock types and aspects of geologic study are well represented. The mountains include an interesting mixture of igneous (both plutonic and volcanic), sedimentary, and metamorphic rocks. Fossils preserved in some of these units, tectonism along major faults defining the mountain front, and the recent extensive glaciation of the higher terrain add to the range's varied and unique geologic history. From sharp granitic peaks rising above glacially scoured basins to lava-capped ridgetops and rushing mountain streams, ancient and ongoing geologic processes are apparent throughout the range.

A Brief Introduction to Geologic Rock Types

Geologists have classified all the earth's rocks into three major types based on the rock's process of origin. These major types are igneous, sedimentary, and metamorphic. **Igneous** rocks form from magma (very hot liquid "rock") originating deep in the interior of the earth. These igneous rocks can be further subdivided depending on whether they reach the earth's surface before cooling and solidifying. Those which reach the surface are considered **volcanic**, and these include lavas such as basalt or andesite (nearly the entire Cascade Range of Oregon is made up of these two types of volcanic rock). Those that cool beneath the surface are considered **plutonic**. The bright, white granitic rocks of the central High Wallowas are plutonic, having cooled miles below the earth's surface more than 150 million years ago. A few types of plutonic rocks include granite, diorite, and gabbro.

The second major rock type is **sedimentary**. These are rocks that form from erosion and weathering of other rocks (limestone is an exception, as it forms from the compaction and crystallization of ancient sea shells). Some sedimentary rocks may contain fossils of leaves, needles, vertebrates, mollusks, or any number of other life forms. These are preserved as the rock forms. Some typical sedimentary rocks include limestone, sandstone, and shale.

The last major rock type is **metamorphic**. These form from pre-existing rocks that have been changed mineralogically and/or texturally through the addition of heat and pressure. These changes are often a result of ongoing and exceedingly slow tectonic processes. Rocks can change, or metamorphose, if they are subject to different pressures or temperatures than they experienced during their initial formation. The mineral assemblage of a rock often indicates a state of equilibrium, meaning certain minerals form and are compatible with one another at certain temperatures and pressures. Chemical reactions take place as a rock is subject to *different* environmental conditions and these reactions change the rock's mineralogy and general appearance. Tectonic processes are able to, over great periods of time, place a rock originally formed at the surface tens of kilometers below the surface. Here the rock is no longer stable mineralogically, and chemical reactions take place to form minerals that are more stable at these greater depths and high temperatures. Then, likely over millions of years, the rock may once again reach the surface through uplift and erosion of any overlying rocks. Some common metamorphic rocks include schist, gneiss, slate, and marble.

All of these three major rock types are represented in the Wallowa Mountains. They are part of a geologic history spanning over 250 million years, from the oldest exposed rocks in the area, the metamorphic Clover Creek Greenstone, to the very recent glacial and fluvial deposits of the last couple of hundred years. Table 3 is an abbreviated geologic time scale applicable to rocks found in the Wallowa Mountains and much of the surrounding region.

Table 3. Geologic Time Scale

Era	Period	Epoch	Time
Cenozoic	Quaternary	Holocene	10,000 yrs – present
		Pleistocene	2 mya – 10,000 yrs
	Tertiary	Pliocene	5 mya – 2 mya
		Miocene	25 mya – 5 mya
		Oligocene	38 mya – 25 mya
		Eocene	55 mya – 38 mya
		Paleocene	65 mya – 55 mya
Mesozoic	Cretaceous		144 mya – 65 mya
	Jurassic		213 mya – 144 mya
	Triassic		248 mya – 213 mya
Paleozoic	Permian		286 mya – 248 mya

Mya= millions of years ago.

The above table only includes time periods represented by rocks of the Wallowa region. The geologic time scale goes much farther back in time to the Archean Eon of the Precambrian, approximately

4.6 billion years ago. Though the geologic evolution of the Wallowa region spans several hundred million years, on the geologic time scale this could be considered fairly recent as some rocks on the surface of the earth are believed to be over 3.8 billion years old.

A brief synthesis of the geologic history of the Wallowa region begins with a chain of volcanoes in the Pacific Ocean. This volcanic chain, termed an **island arc**, periodically erupted between 250 to 270 million years ago. Ash and lava flows covered the slopes of the volcanoes, while sediments were deposited around the flanks of the chain, forming beds of shale, sandstone, and, in the warm tropical waters of the ancient Pacific, limestone. The island arc and its associated rocks, called the **Wallowa Terrane**, drifted via **plate tectonics** across the globe for millions of years, eventually "slamming" into the western margin of North America. The rocks were strongly deformed and altered during the collision process, forming metamorphic rocks. The igneous Wallowa Batholith intruded into this jumble of older rocks prior to and during the collision of the Wallowa Terrane into North America. This **accretion** process ceased about 80 million years ago, and the Wallowa Terrane, whose rocks are exposed throughout much of the Wallowa Mountains, became part of the continent. Initial uplift of the region likely occurred during this period as well.

Later, during the Cenozoic Era, volcanoes erupting to the west in central Oregon covered many parts of the region with ash and lava flows. Although these rocks are not well exposed in the High Wallowas, they can be seen in the depths of nearby Hells Canyon. Uplift of the area again occurred in Miocene time, followed by a period of erosion. Then, beginning approximately 17 million years ago, tremendous lava flows began erupting through a series of long fissures that developed on the northern and eastern margins of the region. These eruptions formed the Columbia River Basalt Group, which covered much of the Wallowa Terrane and most of central and eastern Washington and northern Oregon with enormous amounts of basaltic lava. The eruptions continued sporadically until about 6 million years ago.

The most recent events in the area, which have occurred over the last few million years, include uplift of the present-day Wallowa

Mountains along major faults and extensive glaciation of the range. As recently as 15,000 years ago the Wallowas supported large alpine glaciers many miles in length. Only a few hundred years ago smaller glaciers could be found on some of the higher peaks of the range. Today, there are no longer any active glaciers in the range, though a few small permanent snowfields linger, tucked away in high, shadowy cirques beneath the higher peaks. The evolution of the Wallowa region continues today, as both ongoing geologic processes and climatic fluctuations continue to shape the landscape of the area.

Regional Tectonic Evolution

The theory of Plate Tectonics revolutionized the science of geology in the late 1960s and early 1970s, and this theory has important implications for the geologic evolution of the Wallowa region. The theory essentially states that the crust and upper mantle of the earth form distinct rigid blocks of rock, known as plates, and that these plates "float" on top of a partially molten substrate. The plates comprise the **lithosphere**, while the lower, partially liquid material on which the lithosphere moves is called the **asthenosphere**. The plates of the lithosphere are able to move great distances, over millions of years, "floating" on the asthenosphere.

When lithospheric plates collide, a number of different geologic scenarios may result. One plate can dive beneath the other, forming what is known as a **subduction zone**. This is occurring along the western margin of the Pacific Northwest, where a denser oceanic plate is currently being subducted beneath the North American continent. This has caused melting of rocks beneath these Pacific states, forming hot, liquid rock, termed **magma**. This magma has risen to the surface in several areas forming the high volcanoes and lava plateaus of the Cascade Range, which stretches along the area of the subduction zone from northern California northward for hundreds of miles to southern British Columbia.

If two continental plates collide, they can form a massive and exceptionally high mountain belt. The highest mountains in the world, the Himalaya, were formed by the collision of two continental plates, India and Asia. The density difference between the two plates is slight, and thus the plates have nowhere to go except upward, producing an extensive and extremely high mountainous region. Peaks in the Himalaya commonly exceed 20,000 feet in height, with the tallest, Mt. Everest, topping 29,000 feet.

A third scenario may occur when plates collide; one plate is plastered or **sutured** onto another. This is what occurred in the Wallowa region. A "microplate", the Wallowa Terrane, collided with the much larger North American continental plate, plastering itself onto the older continent. This process is known as **accretion**, and subsequently the Wallowa Terrane microplate is considered an **accreted terrane**. Geologists Tracy Vallier and Howard Brooks, working with other scientists in the area, pioneered the accretion/island arc theory in the region, and today it is widely recognized as the most probable origin of the older rocks in the Wallowas.

The tectonic evolution of the Wallowa Mountains began approximately 120 million years ago, when the western edge of North America was in present-day Idaho. About this time, a small piece of lithosphere, the Wallowa Terrane, was on a collision course with the continental coastline. Eventually the two collided, and the terrane rocks were accreted to the North American **craton** (the "original" continent). The rocks of the craton of North America are mostly between 2 and 3.5 *billion* years old, much older than those of the Wallowa Terrane, which are from 270 to 190 million years old.

The accretion process took approximately 30-40 million years to complete. The area along which collision and accretion took place is known as a **suture zone**. Think of it as a place where the two plates were stitched together. The suture area here is named the Salmon River Suture Zone after its exposures in the Salmon River country of west-central Idaho. It follows a line roughly between the towns of Orofino and Riggins, Idaho.

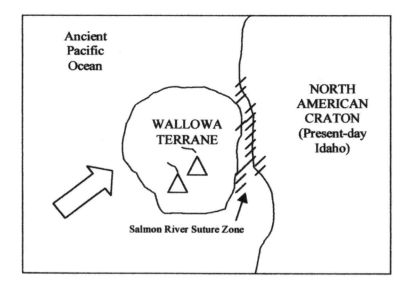

Figure 10. As the Wallowa Terrane collided with and accreted to North America a zone of highly deformed rock, termed the Salmon River Suture Zone, developed marking the boundary between the two "plates".

Much of central and eastern Oregon is a collage of accreted terranes. Some geologists believe that the Wallowa terrane may actually be only a part of a much larger Blue Mountains island arc terrane. Regardless, it is apparent that the rocks of this region are distinctly different from those of the North American craton. A survey of the far western United States reveals numerous exotic terranes scattered along the fringes of the continent. It appears that over time more and more crust has been added to the western margin of North America through the processes of **continental drift** and **plate tectonics**. Fossils preserved within rocks of these terranes differ markedly from those of similar age on the North America craton, further strengthening the idea that the terrane rocks are of a different origin and are only geologically recent additions to this continent.

Following, and perhaps during, the accretion of the Wallowa terrane, initial uplift of the Wallowa region occurred in the late Mesozoic. This uplift, and subsequent erosion, occurred periodically throughout much of the Cenozoic Era (the last 65 million years). Geologists believe the granodiorite core of the High Wallowas, the Wallowa batholith, originally crystallized approximately 15 miles below the surface. However, this pluton was exposed at the surface by Miocene time, as evidenced by its contact with the earlier flows of the Columbia River Basalt Group. This indicates that, in the period of time from the Cretaceous to the Miocene, erosion had removed all of the rocks above the batholith and uplift had brought these rocks to the surface. There lava flows of the Columbia River Basalt Group were deposited on an exposed, weathered surface of granodiorite. This is evidence that, approximately 17 million years ago, during the earlier phases of these eruptions of basalt, the rocks surrounding the plutonic core had been eroded away and the core was then exposed at the surface.

One of the most recent tectonic events of the area is the uplift of the present-day Wallowa Mountains, which occurred during the last few million years. The steep nature of the northern part of the range indicates the current topography of this mountain range is fairly young in terms of geologic time. If the mountains were much older and more heavily eroded, they would form a less abrupt wall, perhaps a broad domal ridge with rounded peaks, like much of the modern Appalachians of the eastern United States. The northern escarpment of the range formed by differential movement along a major fault, the Wallowa fault (Figure 12). A **fault** is a fracture or fracture zone in the earth along which rocks move relative to one another. On a large scale movement along faults often forms major topographic features such as mountains and basins. **Earthquakes** can occur as rocks move along these faults. The rocks north of the Wallowa fault moved down relative to those south of the fault, forming the dramatic mountain front. Moraines of the last glacial period that cross the trace of the fault, such as those along Wallowa Lake, appear to be undisturbed. This indicates that the most recent movement along the fault forming the mountain front likely occurred prior to the last major advances of the Pleistocene glaciers. If activity had occurred following deposition of this glacial debris, it would be apparent in these recent moraines. Northwest-

Figure 11. The fault-bounded northern escarpment of the Wallowas from the Wallowa Valley. The grassy slope extending out from beneath the range's front is a moraine formed by the ancient Wallowa Glacier.

trending faults bound the southern edge of the range as well, though the fault **scarp** produced by movements along these faults isn't quite as abrupt as that of the northern part of the range.

The trace of the Wallowa fault, defining the northern margin of the Wallowa Mountains, is easily visible from the air as a strong linear feature, and is even more pronounced in satellite images taken of the area from space. These images show the dark green and white mountains contrasting sharply with the lighter fields far below on the north side of the fault. The fault is the southeastern extension of a pronounced, large-scale linear geologic feature which extends from the Olympic Mountains of western Washington, across the Cascade Range and the Columbia Basin, to this part of Oregon. The feature has been called the Olympic-Wallowa lineament. There is still much debate as to the origin of this lineament and its significance in the geologic evolution of the Pacific Northwest.

Tectonic activity has also occurred just north of the Wallowas during the last few million years. Pat Spencer and Bob Carson of Whitman College have recently studied an exposed gravel unit in the Wallowa valley which indicates that tectonism occurred along the floor of the Wallowa Valley and to the north during the Pleistocene Epoch. Termed the Enterprise Gravel, it suggests that previously, during the late Pliocene and mid-Pleistocene, the Wallowa River actually flowed due north through the Joseph Upland region. Tectonic uplift of these uplands since the mid-Pleistocene resulted in a drainage reversal and a subsequent realignment of the Wallowa River. Today, several drainages originating in the Joseph Uplands flow south toward the mountain front, and the Wallowa River has shifted its course accordingly, flowing to the northwest toward the Minam and Grande Ronde Rivers.

Rocks of the Wallowa Mountians

The Wallowas contain a fascinating mixture of varying rock types spanning over 250 million years of geologic time. Though there are several distinct units discussed below, some are commonly seen in and about the Wallowas while others are not readily exposed and are largely buried beneath the surface. In the rugged Wallowa country, the rock one is climbing up or walking atop is likely one of five units: the Clover Creek Greenstone, the Martin Bridge Formation, the Hurwal Formation, the Wallowa Batholith, or the Columbia River Basalt Group.

The Wallowa Terrane
The **Clover Creek Greenstone**, the **Martin Bridge Formation**, and the **Hurwal Formation** formed as part of the oceanic volcanic chain known as the **Wallowa Terrane**. These rocks are the oldest found in the region and can be seen throughout much of the Wallowa Mountains, in Hells Canyon, and in the Seven Devils Mountains of Idaho.
Some geologists believe that the Wallowa terrane is a piece of a much larger accreted terrane known as Wrangellia. This terrane, named for the Wrangell Mountains, can be seen in several localities in

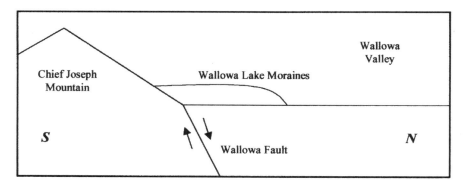

Figure 12. The Wallowa Fault. Uplift of the Wallowas occurred as the rocks south of the fault moved upward relative to those on the north side of the fault. The Wallowa Lake moraines remained undisturbed, indicating that the most recent movement of the Wallowa Fault occurred before deposition of these moraines in the Late Pleistocene.

Alaska and Vancouver Island. Similar fossils found in both the ancient island-arc rocks of Wrangallia and the Wallowa terrane suggest there may be a relationship between the Wallowa rocks and those found far to the north.

Clover Creek Greenstone.   The oldest exposed rocks in the Wallowa Mountains are the lower and upper members of the Clover Creek Greenstone. These rocks comprise much of Chief Joseph Mountain in the northern range, and can be seen readily along the first couple of miles of the West Fork Wallowa River Trail beneath the peak. They also are well exposed in the eastern High Wallowas in the three forks of the Imnaha River and in the Krag Peak/Red Mountain area of the southern range.

The Clover Creek Greenstone in the Wallowas, which is correlative to the Seven Devils Volcanic Group found in Idaho, is Permian and Triassic in age, having formed from 225 to 270 million years ago. Originally lava flows and volcanigenic sedimentary rock (sediments derived from a volcanic source), the rocks have been metamorphosed into greenstone. The rock now has a different mineral composition than the original volcanic rocks from which it was formed.

The lower members of the Clover Creek Greenstone are Permian in age and include the Windy Ridge Formation and the younger Hunsaker Formation.

The upper Clover Creek greenstone is Triassic in age, forming approximately 225 to 240 million years ago, and it consists of two formations: the older Wildsheep Creek Formation and the younger Doyle Creek Formation. Many of the rocks of the Clover Creek Greenstone contain abundant epidote and chlorite minerals, which give the rocks their greenish tint.

Lucile Group:
Martin Bridge Formation and the Hurwal Formation

Lying stratigraphically above the Clover Creek Greenstone is the Upper Triassic to Lower Jurassic **Lucile Group**. These rocks are approximately 190 to 220 million years old and are sedimentary in origin. The Lucile Group includes both the **Martin Bridge Formation** and the **Hurwal Formation**. The Upper Triassic Martin Bridge Formation is predominantly limestone, though in some areas it has been deformed and metamorphosed forming marble. Overlying the Martin Bridge is the Upper Triassic to Lower Jurassic Hurwal Formation, a younger group of shales that also have been locally metamorphosed.

Martin Bridge Formation. The Martin Bridge Formation was recognized and named earlier this century, after an exposure located near a bridge crossing Eagle Creek in the southern Wallowas. The undeformed and unmetamorphosed Martin Bridge limestone found at this type locality at the southern margin of the range is characteristically dark gray to black and fine grained, quite unlike most exposures in the heart of the range. This limestone formed in a warm, tropical environment along the periphery of the volcanic chain of the Wallowa

Figure 13. A cirque on the southeast side of the Matterhorn reveals folded marble of the Martin Bridge Formation (light-colored rock of cliff face) overlying darker rocks of the Hurwal Formation. ⟶

Terrane many millions of years ago during the Triassic (see Figure 15 below). Carbonate (limestone is calcium carbonate) rocks are common in these environments, and present-day limestone reefs can be seen in the Caribbean and other shallow, marine environments near the equator. Limestone is usually a light gray to white color but this limestone contains some carbon, darkening the appearance of the rock. Fossils are fairly abundant in the Martin Bridge, and have been used to help date the formation.

The Martin Bridge Formation has been locally metamorphosed and deformed, likely by tectonic processes associated with accretion of the Wallowa Terrane. The limestone was subjected to stress and higher temperatures and pressures, causing it to metamorphose into marble. This recrystallized rock is characteristically coarse-grained and is a white to gray color unlike the darker gray and black of the undisturbed Martin Bridge seen in other localities. Most of the Martin Bridge in the heart of the range is highly contorted, light-colored marble.

Much of the Martin Bridge contains fossils. Ancient fossilized marine life, including bivalves, ammonites, conodonts, and corals, has been excavated from the limestone. These creatures lived in the warm, subtropical waters of the central Pacific along the fringes of the Wallowa island arc many millions of years ago. In addition to these fossils, a fairly well preserved ichthyosaur has also been found and excavated from the rock unit. Ichthyosaurs are streamlined, fish-like reptiles that lived in marine environments from the Middle Triassic to the Late Cretaceous.

Spectacular exposures of the Martin Bridge Formation occur in the Matterhorn-Sacajawea area and near Hawkins Pass in the central range. At these locations intense folding of the rock is apparent. Many of the dark folded bands mixed in with the light marble are older dikes cutting through the Martin Bridge Formation which were deformed along with the marble millions of years ago. Much of the

Figure 14. Slopes of the Hurwal Divide rise abruptly above the clear waters of Ice Lake. ——→

headwater regions of the three forks of the Imnaha River are under-lain by Martin Bridge, and it can also be seen near Aneroid Lake and above the East Fork Eagle Creek valley in the southern part of the range.

Hurwal Formation. The Hurwal Formation, the younger member of the Lucile Group, lies above the Martin Bridge Formation and is Late Triassic to Early Jurassic in age. It is predominantly made up of dark gray to brownish red shale, which formed as sediments from the volcanic chain were deposited in the surrounding ocean (Figure 15). The formation has been metamorphosed in many areas. The rusty-red hue of the rock in some areas is due to the oxidation of the iron oxide mineral pyrite. The original bedding of the Hurwal remains evident and the rocks contain some well-preserved fossils. Exposures of the Hurwal Formation can be seen around the Frances Lake/Twin Peaks area, along the Hurricane Divide, along the Hurwal Divide (for which it was named), and on Sentinel Peak and Pete's Point. In the East Fork Eagle Creek valley the Hurwal Formation lies below the Martin Bridge Formation on the valley walls. How can this be if the Martin Bridge is the older of the two units? It appears that the original horizontal bedding of the rocks has been overturned by tremendous faulting, resulting in an inverted time sequence where the older rocks of the Martin Bridge actually lie on top of the younger Hurwal Formation.

The Wallowa Batholith

The whitish, "salt and pepper" speckled rock so common in much of the central and western High Wallowas is **granodiorite**. Granodiorite is a rock of the granitic family that is intermediate in mineral composition between granite and diorite (hence its name). This crystalline rock forms the bright landscape of the scenic Lakes Basin below Eagle Cap. Among other places, it also comprises much of the stunning glacial valleys and sharp peaks along the three forks of Eagle Creek, the area near Cornucopia, and many of the creek and river valley floors of the western part of the range.

The granodiorite of the range solidified slowly beneath the earth's surface, forming a body of rock known as a **pluton**. A **batholith**

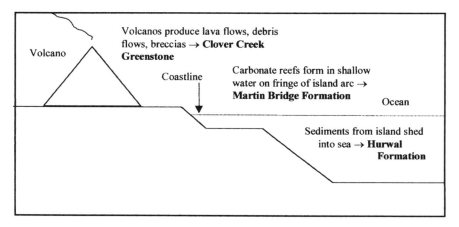

Figure 15. Paleoenvironments of the Wallowa Terrane, showing likely depositional environments of the three Wallowa Terrane rock units.

is a large pluton covering an area greater than 100 km². The granodiorite of this area comprises a great body of rock known as the Wallowa Batholith. In contrast to a volcanic eruption, magma can form deep inside the earth and crystallize before reaching the surface, and this is how the granodiorite of the Wallowa Batholith formed. Later, uplift along faults and erosion of the overlying rocks exposed this once deeply buried pluton (see Figure 16).

The Wallowa Batholith crystallized at least 10 miles below the earth's surface from 160-140 million years ago. The pluton intruded into the older rocks of the Wallowa Terrane (the Clover Creek Greenstone, Martin Bridge Formation, and the Hurwal Formation). The introduction of heat, stress, and water associated with emplacement of the molten rock caused local metamorphism and deformation of the surrounding rocks. Some smaller but related plutonic bodies, known as **stocks**, also intruded into the region during this time. The Sawtooth stock to the north and the Cornucopia stock in the south are smaller magma bodies closely related to the larger Wallowa Batholith.

As mentioned previously, the rock of the Wallowa Batholith is not truly granite, but consists of a number of rock types of the granitic

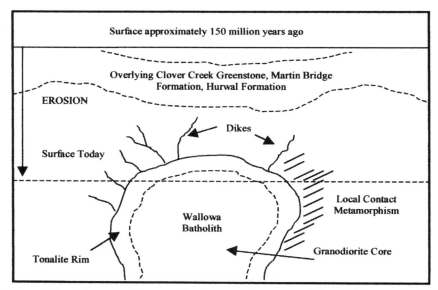

Figure 16. Schematic diagram showing emplacement of the Wallowa Batholith beneath the surface approximately 150 million years ago. Dikes, usually rich in water and valuable elements such as gold, silver, or copper, squeeze up into fractures in the overlying rock. As erosion occurs, the batholith and dikes may eventually be exposed, and the dikes may be mined as lode deposits. An aureole of contact metamorphism surrounds the batholith, as the overlying rock is changed mineralogically due to the addition of heat and often an influx of water from the cooling magma.

family. The batholith is **zoned**, meaning the interior of the batholith is mineralogically different than the borders of the pluton. A zone of slightly different rock often develops on the rim of plutons, as temperatures differ (it is cooler) from that within the magma body (Figure 16). In the case of the Wallowa Batholith tonalite rims the pluton whereas the core is granodiorite. Tonalite consists largely of the light-colored plagioclase feldspar, glassy-looking quartz, and biotite and hornblende, which are darker colored, giving the rocks a salt and pepper look upon closer inspection. Granodiorite includes the above minerals but also a significant amount of potassium feldspar, which is minimal or absent in tonalite, distinguishing the two rock types. Most of the exposed Wallowa Batholith is granodiorite. As plutons cool, residual fluids, rich with water and incompatible elements such as gold and silver, are the last to crystallize into solid rock. These fluids shoot up through the surrounding solidified rocks, forming dikes. Dikes of aplite (a sugary looking fine-grained rock) and pegmatite (a coarse-grained rock of predominantly quartz and potassium feldspar) cut through the main batholith in some areas.

The tremendous heat of the pluton, perhaps 850°C, caused local **contact metamorphism** of the surrounding older country rock. Contact metamorphism differs from **regional metamorphism** in that it is generally confined to a very small area, measurable in tens of feet or less. This is in contrast to large-scale regional metamorphism that can affect hundreds of square miles of rock. Contact metamorphism is commonly associated with plutonic bodies that locally increase temperatures, leading to mineralogic changes in the surrounding rock. Heat and water are key ingredients in driving chemical reactions, and the Wallowa Batholith had enough of both of these to alter rocks along its margins. The available heat to drive chemical reactions quickly diminishes farther away from the batholith, and the metamorphism of the surrounding rocks quickly decreases accordingly until eventually the pluton has no discernible effect on the rock around it. An excellent exposure of a contact-metamorphosed limestone, termed **skarn**, can be seen just to the south of Aneroid Lake at the head of the East Fork Wallowa River canyon. Here one can actually walk along and see where the pluton intruded the older rocks of the Martin Bridge Formation.

Rocks of the granitic family (granite, granodiorite, tonalite, etc.) can produce some of nature's most elegant and beautiful landscapes, as these rocks often weather into clean, brilliant spires, large, rounded boulders, or smooth, sculpted outcrops. The combination of granitic rock and ice has produced some of the most spectacular scenery in the mountain West; the massive walls and heavenly domes of the Sierra Nevada, the sharp crests and clear alpine tarns of Idaho's Sawtooths, the high tablelands and serrated peaks of the Wind River Range, all are the result of ice sculpting granite. In parts of the Wallowas, the exposed granodiorite of the Wallowa Batholith and the range's ancient rivers of ice have combined to form yet another striking mountain

Figure 17. A view of Eagle Cap rising above Mocassin Lake in the Lakes Basin.

landscape. One area of the range underlain by granitic rock, the Lakes Basin, a small plateau beneath the north face of Eagle Cap, is particularly spectacular, and is understandably the most visited region in the range. For here one finds clear bubbling streams, cold, glassy lakes, lush, green meadows, and scattered groves of pine and fir, all set in a brilliant landscape of bright crystalline rock. Similar to John Muir's Range of Light on a clear day, this Wallowa landscape sometimes seems to be composed of light, the rocks, the sky, the water, the boughs of the firs and pines all illuminated by a rich sunlight. Though the magma of the Wallowa Batholith may have cooled deep below the earth's surface over a hundred million years ago, today its radiant crystals form what many consider the most beautiful part of the Wallowa Mountains.

Mining

Plutons of granite and granodiorite, such as the Wallowa Batholith, are important to economic geologists. The intrusion of these magma bodies often results in intense **mineralization** of the surrounding rock as well as crystallization of rare elements in dikes associated with the plutons. Precious metals such as gold, silver, and copper are often found near plutonic bodies.

The Wallowa Mountains are dotted with numerous mining prospects, most of which were more active earlier this century. In the late 1800s and early 1900s, several mines were operating in the Wallowas as well as the Greenhorn and Elkhorn ranges to the west. The Cornucopia Mining District, in the southern Wallowas, produced more than 15 million dollars worth of gold in the 1930s and 40s. Gold, silver, and copper were the primary minerals mined in the Wallowas, though marble and limestone has also been mined in the region as well.

Metals were either mined as **lode deposits** or placer deposits. Lode deposits are those which are mined in place as part of the bedrock. Extensive tunnels may be built in the sides of mountains to mine the ore. **Placer deposits** are those which are mined in stream gravels. Over time erosion of a lode deposit can remove some of the minerals and redeposit them in stream channels. Water sorts and deposits debris by size and weight, so heavy minerals such as gold and silver may be concentrated in parts of a channel and can be mined by dredging along the streambed.

Many mining prospects are scattered throughout the Wallowas both inside and outside the Eagle Cap Wilderness boundary. Copper is the most abundant metal found in the area, with significant concentrations occurring in the Aneroid Lake basin, McCully Basin, Copper Creek basin, and near Hawkins Pass. The major occurrences are in tactite zones along the contact between the plutonic granodiorite and the older limestone. Others minerals found in these zones include chalcopyrite and malachite. Copper minerals have also been found disseminated in limy beds of the Hurwal Formation. Significant concentrations of silver have been found in quartz veins on Chief Joseph Mountain. The only important nonmetallic resource of the area is the limestone of the Martin Bridge Formation, a potential source of calcium carbonate for lime and cement. The Black Marble quarry at the northern end of the range operated intermittently from the 1920s through the 1950s, mining the beautiful black marble of the Martin Bridge Formation.

The Cenozoic Rocks

Long after the development and accretion of the Wallowa Terrane and emplacement of the Wallowa Batholith several more rock units were deposited in the region. These are rocks of the most recent geologic era, the Cenozoic, which spans the last 65 million years of the Earth's history.

Clarno Formation. The Clarno Formation, Eocene and Oligocene in age, marks the beginning of rocks that formed and were deposited during the Cenozoic. The source of the lava, mud flows, and sediments of this unit is still not well understood but it appears the volcanic rocks were erupted along the western fringe of the Blue Mountain region. Many of the colorful sedimentary units of the Clarno formation contain abundant fossils. Avocado, fig, and numerous nut fossils have been preserved in the formation as well as fossils of large mammals. As evidenced by the variety of life preserved in the rocks, the climate of eastern Oregon was subtropical during this period. The Clarno Formation is well exposed at the western edge of the Blue Mountains, most notably along the John Day River in the Clarno Unit of John Day Fossil Beds National Monument, but is not readily seen in the Wallowas.

John Day Formation. The John Day Formation overlies the Clarno, and is Oligocene and Miocene in age. Both the Clarno and John Day Formations are not seen in the Wallowa Mountains, as uplift of the range likely caused erosion and removal of these rocks from the range. These units may underlie other formations on the periphery of the range however.

The John Day Formation includes volcanics and volcanigenic sediments. The source of these units was a series of volcanoes that erupted between the western edge of the Blues and the Cascade crest. Many of these volcanoes erupted silica-rich lavas such as **rhyolite**. Large amounts of gas within these magmas led to violent eruptions that produced hot, incandescent clouds of ash know as **ignimbrites**. These moved rapidly across the landscape incinerating everything in their path. Rapid deposition of volcanic ash and the subsequent erosion and redeposition of these units in lakes and riverbeds facilitated preservation of lifeforms living in the area as fossils. The soft and colorful mud and ash layers of the John Day Formation can be seen in scattered localities in east-central Oregon, most notably on the beautiful Painted Hills of the John Day Fossil Beds National Monument.

Tertiary Gravel Unit. A mysterious Tertiary gravel is exposed at a few sites within the Wallowas, though the deposit is only well exposed along Jim White Ridge in the western range. The gravel includes very well rounded boulders, some of which are 2 feet in diameter, and appears to be fluvial in origin. In most of the deposits 90% or more of the boulders are quartzite, though in one location south of Cached Lake the gravels include rocks from the older Triassic units found in other parts of the range. The source of the quartzite is not known. Gneissic rocks similar to those found in west-central Idaho also make up a small portion of the gravel, and it is possible these rocks were deposited in the Wallowa region prior to more recent uplift and, significantly, before the formation of Hells Canyon. Placer gold has been reported on Jim White Ridge in association with this curious gravel unit.

Columbia River Basalt Group. The Columbia River Basalt Group is the dark reddish brown, horizontally layered lavas found on some of the higher peaks of the central and eastern Wallowas and covering most of the ridgetops of the western range. They also are quite evident in the rugged Grande Ronde, Joseph, Imnaha, and Snake River canyons of the surrounding region, where they form steep, step-like slopes dropping thousands of feet to the canyon floors.

The lavas of the Columbia River Basalt Group (CRBG) are considered flood basalts. They erupted in such huge volumes that they produced floods of molten rock that in time covered hundreds of square miles of the Inland Northwest. The lavas blanket much of central and eastern Washington and northern Oregon, forming what is known as the Columbia Plateau. The basalts erupted from long fissures in the earth's crust from about 17 to roughly 6 million years ago. Approximately 85% of the total volume of the entire group erupted during a short time interval known as the Grande Ronde period. This

Figure 18. Layer-cake basalt of the Columbia River Basalt Group tops a peak near the headwaters of Big Sheep Creek.

period of intense activity occurred from about 17.5 to 15.5 million years ago. The present day site of the Wallowa Mountains, and extending to the north, is where the fissures feeding the eruptions developed. Enormous amounts of lava erupted through cracks in the Earth's crust, termed **dikes** (see Figure 19). Dikes of the Chief Joseph Dike Swarm cut right through the older rocks of the Wallowa Mountains (the Wallowa Batholith and Wallowa Terrane rocks). These dark brownish-red streaks of basalt are particularly conspicuous in the High Wallowas where they cut through the lighter-colored rocks of the Wallowa Batholith and the Martin Bridge Formation. They can be seen criss-crossing the higher parts of the range in many places.

The reason for the development of the often 50 mile-long fissures that were the source for the lavas and the accompanying enormous volume of lava extruded remains elusive to geologists studying these flood basalts. The eruptions may have been related to **subduction** occurring

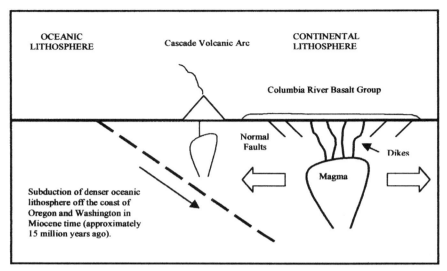

Figure 19. Diagram showing back-arc extension behind the active Cascade Volcanic Arc and eruption of the Columbia River flood basalts through feeder dikes near the Oregon-Washington-Idaho border. The crust behind the Cascade arc was being pulled apart (as indicated by the large arrows), leading to normal faulting and eruption of the lava.

far to the west along the coastal margin of Oregon and Washington in Miocene time. Sometimes when oceanic lithosphere is subducted beneath another plate, the sinking of the downgoing slab may cause the overriding plate to extend. To compensate for this pull-apart motion, the overriding plate may break up, forming fractures through which lava could rise and reach the surface. This is termed **back-arc extension**, meaning the crust is being extended behind an active volcanic arc, in this case the Cascade Range (Figure 19). This has been noted in other regions of the world and is currently one explanation for the origin of the flood basalts of the Columbia Plateau.

Another possible and perhaps more plausible explanation for the eruption of the Columbia River Basalt Group is passage of what is termed the Yellowstone "hot spot" beneath this area during the Miocene. The Yellowstone hot spot is a distinctive "plume" of magma that today drives volcanic activity in the Yellowstone region of

Wyoming, Idaho, and Montana. (A similar plume feature is the source of the spectacular volcanic chain of Hawaii in the middle of the Pacific Ocean.) This plume has remained stationary over millions of years of geologic time, while the North American continent has been slowly moving across it, leaving a trace of volcanic activity in its wake. Beginning approximately 17 million years ago the area of northeastern Oregon and west-central Idaho cut by the Chief Joseph Dike Swarm may have passed over the hot spot, leading to enormous volcanic eruptions and the deposition of the Columbia River flood basalts. The trace of the hotspot swings southward onto the Snake River Plain before arcing upward to Yellowstone, where it is active today and producing that area's fascinating hydrothermal and volcanic features. Geologists have noted that the volcanic rocks become progressively younger in age from west (the Columbia River basalts) to east (the lavas of the Snake River Plain and more recently the volcanism of Yellowstone), suggesting periodic expressions of the hot spot over millions of years of geologic time.

The eruptions of the Columbia River Basalt Group are not only notable for their immense volume (some flows contain 3000 cubic kilometers of lava) but also for the great distances some of the flows traveled. The lavas cover nearly all of central and eastern Washington (to depths of 5 km [3 miles] in the Pasco Basin) and northern Oregon. Amazingly, outcrops of the CRBG can also be found as far away as the southern Willamette Valley and along the central Oregon coastline. This means that some of these lava flows somehow traveled nearly 600 km (373 miles) from their source vents in eastern Washington and Oregon or west-central Idaho, through the Columbia River gorge, all the way to the Pacific Ocean. These flows are some of the longest lava flows yet found on the surface of the earth. Though these flood basalts are among the most studied in the world, there is still some debate concerning the cause of the eruptions and how the lavas were able to travel such great distances. Some argue that high eruption rates, coupled with the fluidity of the flows, enabled the lava to pour across the landscape for many hundreds of miles, being "pushed" from behind by the continuous eruption of more magma.

Figure 20. Aneroid Mountain is largely composed of lavas of the Columbia River Basalt Group.

Minerals comprising the basalts include abundant plagioclase feldspar, some pyroxenes, hornblende, biotite, and occasionally a little olivine. The rock is actually a dark gray or black, but exposed surfaces have been weathered changing the rock's appearance. Just as old cars and nails rust, the iron minerals in these rocks have been oxidized, forming a mineral called hematite which gives the rock its red color. Another mineral formed from this weathering process is limonite, which gives the rock a yellowish-brown look.

The horizontally layered basalt flows have been used to estimate the relative displacement along the Wallowa fault bordering the northern part of the range. The same lava flows found on top of Aneroid Mountain at 9700 feet and the far northern Hurricane Divide can be seen at a much lower elevation in the Imnaha River canyon northeast of Enterprise. Assuming the flows were deposited in a layer-cake fashion across relatively flat terrain, this difference in elevation of the same lavas indicates that relative movement along the Wallowa fault is likely over 7000 feet, as the area south of the fault rose above that to the north (Figure 21).

Exposures of the Columbia River Basalt Group can be seen on and near Aneroid Mountain, Ruby Peak, and China Cap in the High Wallowas as well as along the ridges of much of the canyon country of the lower western part of the range. An interesting isolated basalt remnant can be seen on Brown Mountain near Minam Lake in the central range. To the east, many of the steep valley walls of Hells Canyon are composed of lavas of the group.

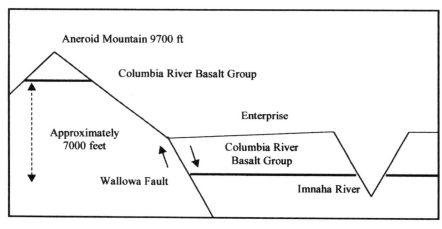

Figure 21. Diagram showing lava flow atop Aneroid Mountain and the same flow exposed in the Imnaha River Canyon northeast of Enterprise. Movement of the Wallowa Fault has been at least 7000 feet since the deposition of this lava as indicated by the displacement of the flow.

Quaternary Deposits

Some of the youngest rock units in the area have not yet lithified into a solid coherent rock. Fluvial and glacial deposits have been laid down during the last few million years of the Quaternary Period, which includes the Pleistocene Epoch and the Holocene Epoch. Also during the Holocene, light colored ash from the eruption of Mt. Mazama (Crater Lake) showered the region approximately 6500 years ago, forming rich soils in some of the region's canyons. **Fluvial** deposits are those associated with rivers and creeks. These include gravel bars and sandy deposits that form along waterways. Many glacially derived deposits, associated with the geologically recent extensive glaciation of the range, can be seen throughout the range.

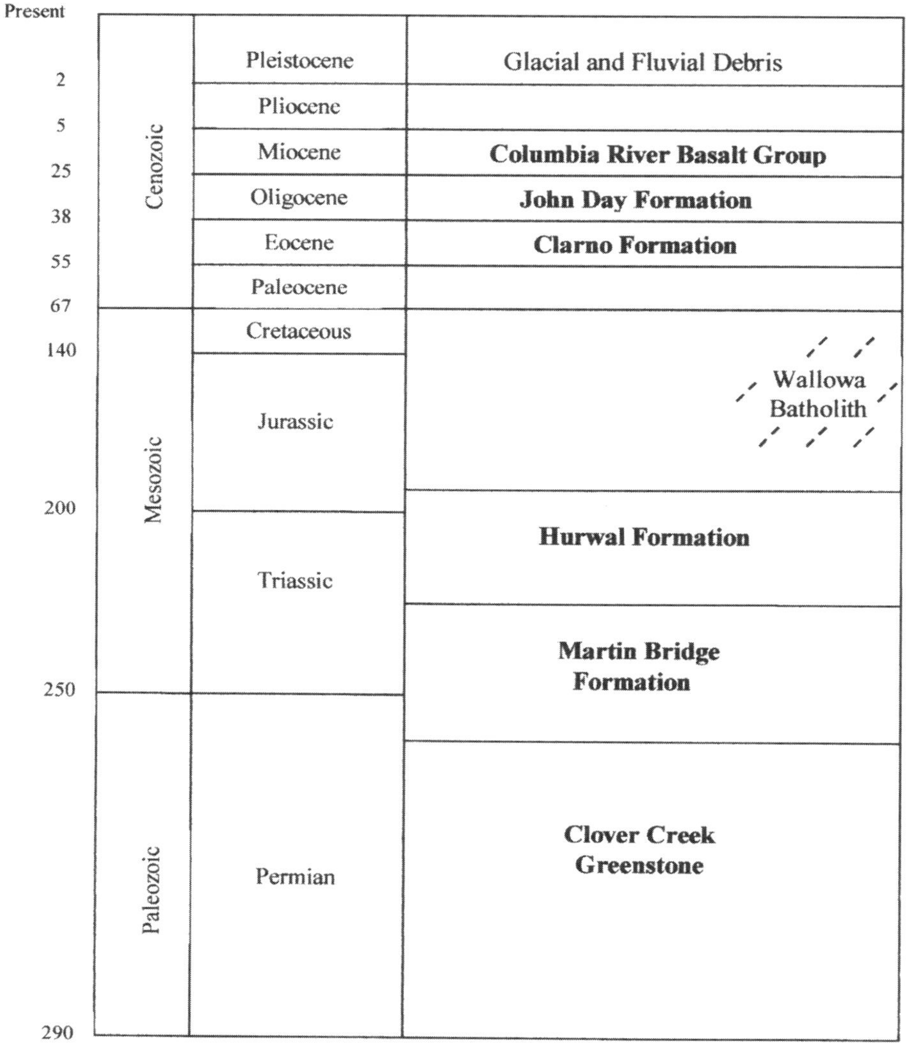

Present			
2	Cenozoic	Pleistocene	Glacial and Fluvial Debris
5		Pliocene	
25		Miocene	**Columbia River Basalt Group**
38		Oligocene	**John Day Formation**
55		Eocene	**Clarno Formation**
67		Paleocene	
140	Mesozoic	Cretaceous	
		Jurassic	*Wallowa Batholith*
200			
		Triassic	**Hurwal Formation**
250			**Martin Bridge Formation**
	Paleozoic	Permian	**Clover Creek Greenstone**
290			

Figure 22. Simplified stratigraphic column of rock units of the Wallowa Mountains including the intrusive Wallowa Batholith. Oldest rocks are at the bottom.

Glacial Geology

Much of the dramatic topography of the Wallowa Mountains can be attributed to the intense erosive work of glaciers. These bodies of moving ice have easily played the most significant role in shaping the stark alpine scenery we see today. The mountains have been subject to repeated episodes of glaciation within the last two million years, and the range has been so strongly eroded by ice that much of it is scoured bedrock lacking any surficial cover. The sharp ridge crests, lake-filled basins, and deep U-shaped valleys of the High Wallowas are characteristic of glaciated regions, and many other glacial features can be seen in the higher parts of the range as well. Today only remnant snow or ice patches remain on the high peaks. Perhaps in time changes in local climate will once again facilitate the formation of large glaciers, which so recently, in terms of geologic time, covered the range in a thick mantle of ice.

As snow accumulates in certain areas over time, and if summers are not warm enough to consistently melt the previous winter's snowfall, bodies of permanent snow and ice may form. If this ice accumulates to a significant thickness, it may form a **glacier** and begin to slowly flow downhill. One can sometimes distinguish a glacier from a snowfield by the presence of **crevasses**, deep clefts in the ice which form as the ice mass moves over the underlying bedrock. These crevasses are indicative of movement, though they may not be visible until late in the summer or early fall when the previous winter's snow has melted revealing these cracks. Crevasses can be over a hundred feet deep on larger glaciers. Water, especially frozen water, is a powerful erosive agent, and given time glaciers are rather easily able to pluck, abrade, crack, and pound bedrock into boulders and fine glacial flour.

Over the course of the earth's history glaciers originating at the poles or in high mountain ranges have advanced and retreated numerous times. The most recent major advances were during the Pleistocene Epoch, a period of time beginning 2 million years ago and ending roughly 10,000 years ago. During the Late Pleistocene, a period from 22,000 to about 15,000 years ago known as the

Figure 23. Krag Peak rises over 4000 feet above the spectacular U-shaped valley of East Eagle Creek.

Wisconsin, much of western North America, and in fact most of the continent, experienced a much cooler and slightly wetter climate. This change in climate allowed extensive **alpine** glaciers to form on most of the higher ranges of the western United States. Also during this period huge masses of continental ice covered most of Canada and the northern United States, extending from western Washington across the continent to the Great Lakes region and into New England.

Many of Oregon's highest mountains were covered by glacial ice during the Wisconsin period. Glaciers blanketed the higher volcanic cones along the spine of the Cascade Range from Mt. Hood to Mt. McLoughlin in southern Oregon. Even 9,700 foot Steens Mountain in the now quite arid Basin and Range supported large valley glaciers at this time. In the Blues, the Elkhorn and Strawberry ranges were glaciated during this period, but the Wallowa Mountains easily had the largest extent of glacial ice in the mountain complex.

This period of cooler and wetter weather led to the development of a large alpine ice cap that covered nearly all of the High Wallowas. This broad area of ice included **lobe or tongue glaciers** that flowed out of the mountains, some extending out into the flat basins below the range. The fingers of ice radiating out of the range were often 20 or more miles long. The glacier forming the Lostine River valley was the longest of the 15 or so that carved out the many characteristically U-shaped valleys of the range. This ancient ice cap was likely similar to some found today in the Coast Ranges and Rocky Mountains of Canada, where glaciers many miles long flow from ice caps out into broad basins below.

A major area of ice accumulation in the range during the Wisconsin period was the Lakes Basin and the drainages extending to the north. A large **neve field**, an area of snow and ice accumulation that feeds glaciers, formed in the Lakes Basin below the north face of Eagle Cap. This body of snow and ice was the main source for the East Fork Lostine, Hurricane, and West Fork Wallowa glaciers. This neve field supplied abundant ice to these three glaciers, with most of the ice spilling to the east down into the area near present-day Frazier Lake and then abruptly turning to the north down the West Fork Wallowa canyon. The Wallowa glacier reached a maximum thickness of nearly 2000 feet as evidenced by the large moraines near Wallowa Lake and the glacial scouring high up on the valley walls of the West Fork Wallowa River canyon. The area near Aneroid Lake fed the East Fork Wallowa glacier, which added additional ice to the main Wallowa glacier just above Wallowa Lake. The Wallowa glacier and the Hurricane glacier were the only two glaciers to advance out past the mountain front, depositing large moraines in the broad Wallowa valley below. The Lostine glacier, over 22 miles long, was longer than both the Hurricane and Wallowa glaciers but did not advance past the mountain front, as the Lostine valley is much longer than those to the east. The large tongues of ice that flowed down the Minam, Lostine, Hurricane, Wallowa, Imnaha, Pine, and Eagle valleys reached some very low elevations, the Pine glacier reaching the lowest, terminating at 3000 feet.

Table 5. Holocene Glaciation of the Wallowa Mountains

Classification	Advance/Retreat	Time
	(this century)	<125yrs ago to present
Neoglacial	Eagle Cap	600 to < 125 yrs ago
	Prospect Lake	950 to 1900 yrs ago
	(Altithermal)	4000 to 6000 yrs ago
Pre-Altithermal	Glacier Lake	6,600 to 12,000 yrs ago

(adapted from Allen, 1975)

Major climate changes, including dramatic increases in annual temperatures and a decrease in precipitation, brought the Wisconsin glaciation to an end approximately 15,000 years ago. During this transition period the huge ice rivers of the range retreated far up into the mountains before disappearing altogether. The end of the Wisconsin glacial period roughly marks the beginning of the Holocene period, a time of warmer temperatures and drier weather for the western United States and for much of the world. The Holocene spans the last 10,000 years and is considered an interglacial period within the current Pleistocene Ice Age. Smaller glacial advances of the more recent **Neoglaciation** have been recognized in the Wallowas and other ranges in the West. About 8,000 years ago, 2,000 years ago, and from about 1350-1850 A.D., ice masses formed and advanced in the higher regions of the range. Table 5 shows names and approximate dates of Holocene glacial advances for the Wallowa Mountains.

These Holocene glaciers were not nearly as extensive as those of the late Pleistocene, but significant alpine cirque glaciers did develop. Moraines of the very recent Eagle Cap advance are considered to be a result of what scientists term the Little Ice Age, a 300-500 year period of cooler, wetter weather which ended in the late 1800s. Since the turn of the century many glaciers in the Pacific Northwest have shrunk drastically, including what was recently Oregon's largest, Collier glacier in the Three Sisters (Eliot glacier on the north side of Mt.Hood is now considered the state's largest). Eagle Cap deposits and those of the older Glacier Lake advance are quite common in the highest cirques of the range, but glacial debris of the Prospect Lake advance is not as apparent. Post-Altithermal advances and subsequent moraines are considered Neoglacial, while the Glacier Lake advance is considered pre-Altithermal. The Altithermal (sometimes called the Hypsithermal) was a period of warmer and drier climatic conditions in the Holocene from about 6,000 to 4,000 years ago. Scientists, mostly through study of soils and tree pollen, have concluded that the climate during this perios was warmer than that of today. It appears from the study of paleoclimates that the earth's climatic regime is not constant, but rather highly variable over periods of time much longer than a human's life span.

Despite the range's abundant snowfall, the Wallowas today have no active glaciers and only a few permanent snowfields. These patches of snow and ice are most often found on the north and northeast facing slopes of the higher peaks, where the predominant winds from the southwest deposit large amounts of windblown snow in deep depressions on lee slopes. These aspects also receive very little direct sunlight, keeping temperatures down and enabling pockets of snow to remain throughout the year. Today's climate of fairly warm summers and the abundance of sunshine between storms in this part of Oregon apparently prevent formation of significant glacial ice. The Benson snowfield, which lies just to the southeast of Eagle Cap in a stark, alpine cirque above Glacier Lake, was very recently (early 1930s) eastern Oregon's only glacier. This mass of ice, shaded by a prominent satellite peak of Eagle Cap, Glacier Peak, has shrunk considerably during the latter half of this century, and is considered stagnant as it no longer shows the crevasse patterns characteristic of active glaciers.

Glacial Landforms

Often sitting below bodies of permanent snow and ice in the range, and scattered about at elevations as low as 4000 feet, one can see large, conspicuous piles of boulders, gravel, and dirt. These are glacial features called **moraines**. A moraine forms at the snout of a glacier or along its sides as bedrock is ground up, transported downslope, and

Figure 24. The north side of Needlepoint from Pop Creek. Note the large moraine extending form right to left beneath the peak's cliff face.

redeposited below the glacier front or along its margins. A moraine forming at the toe of a glacier is called a **terminal moraine**. The fresh appearance of steep-sided terminal moraines in the higher regions of the Wallowas suggests that the now stagnant snowfields above these features were active glaciers only recently, perhaps 200-300 years ago during the Little Ice Age. These **Neoglacial** moraines are most evident near Glacier Lake below the Benson snowfield (the large piles of loose rubble as one looks across the lake toward the peak) and at the base of a small, steep patch of snow and ice below the sheer northeast face of the Matterhorn. These relatively young Neoglacial features are common below many shrinking glaciers and stagnant snowfields throughout the higher ranges of the West.   A different type of moraine, a **lateral moraine**, forms along the sides of a glacier as eroded rock debris is deposited in long ridges. The grassy ridges bordering the sides of Wallowa Lake are text-book examples. These moraines formed as the huge Wallowa Glacier

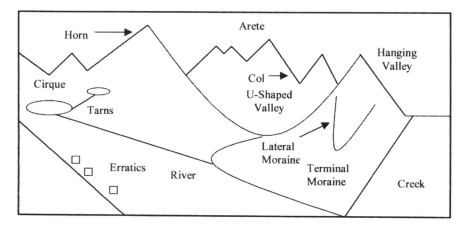

Figure 25. Schematic diagram showing common glacial landforms of the High Wallowas.

eroded and redeposited large amounts of rock and glacial flour along its flanks. A series of long lateral moraines occur on the east side of the lake. These get progressivley older further from the lake, but all are much older than the previously mentioned Neoglacial moraines.

Many of the other landforms seen in the Wallowas today are typical of glaciated areas. One of the most common of these glacial landforms is the **cirque**, a deep, steep-sided basin with a concave floor which forms as glaciers erode the surrounding rock and deposit it downslope. If the glaciers melt and this process of erosion terminates, one is left with a scoured-out, bowl-shaped depression. Any previous drainage system which may have existed prior to glaciation is gone, and these low areas often collect meltwater from existing snowfields, forming today's subalpine and alpine lakes. Ice Lake, Glacier Lake, Frazier Lake, and most of the other lakes scattered about the range may be different shapes and sizes, but nearly all are in cirque basins and of glacial origin.

Where cirque or valley glaciers develop on opposing sides of a ridge or mountain, the glaciers may gradually erode backward towards one another, forming a sharp-crested wall of rock between them, called an **arête**. A typical example would be the Hurwal Divide near

Figure 26. Aneroid Lake occupies a massive cirque at the head of the East Fork of the Wallowa River.

Ice Lake, where glaciers in the Ice Lake basin and the Thorp Creek drainage carved out cirques and troughs to the north and south, leaving this spectacular divide. Sometimes the walls separating the ice masses may be eroded all the way through, and the glaciers can then coalesce and form what is called a col. Many passes in the Wallowas, such as Polaris and Hawkins, are cols.

As cirque glaciers erode every side of a mountain, an isolated steep-sided remnant of rock may be spared, forming a pyramid-shaped peak, or **horn** (Figure 29). Notable examples of these spectacular features include the famous Matterhorn of Switzerland and Mt. Assiniboine in the Canadian Rockies. Horns in the Wallowas include Needle Point, Cusick Mountain, and Sacajawea.

A common glacial landform in the Wallowas and many other ranges of the western United States is the **U-shaped valley** or **glacial trough**. As large valley glaciers move downslope and erode bedrock, they can form deep, smooth-sided troughs with a characteristic cross-section

Figure 27. Arete extending from the col of Hawkins Pass.

shaped like a U. The valley walls of these deep glacial troughs are commonly thousands of feet high. All the major drainages in the Wallowas are U-shaped valleys, evidence of the work of large glaciers during the Wisconsin period.

Many smaller valleys along the sides of the major crests of the range begin as relatively gentle alpine basins, but soon they steepen considerably, the meltwater draining these areas quickly dropping thousands of feet into the previously mentioned deep glacial troughs of the range's major drainages. These high perched basins are glacial features known as **hanging valleys**. As huge glaciers filled the principle drainages with thousands of feet of ice, smaller tributary ice masses fed into the main glaciers off of surrounding ridges. When the large valley glaciers melted, smaller glacial basins were left stranded high up on the valley walls. These hanging valleys often form perpendicular to the paths of the major glaciers, and a quick look at a topographic map can reveal many hanging valleys throughout the range, including the Ice Lake and Glacier Lake basins. Thus the region where these hanging valleys steepen considerably often marks the upper limit of the ice which occupied the major drainages. Study of these hanging valleys and lateral moraines situated high up on the sides of the range's major U-shaped valleys indicate the rivers of ice draining the Wallowa highlands during the Wisconsin glaciation were at least two thousand feet thick.

No where is the work of the ancient glaciers of the Wallowas more apparent than near the Matterhorn and Sacajawea, the two highest peaks in the range. On a cold, clear morning in mid-October, while camping beneath the huge marble walls of these peaks in the Hurricane Creek valley, several friends and I decided to see if we could somehow get up to the top of the Matterhorn from this western side. We had climbed the peak from Ice Lake many times (it is actually just a moderate hike), but on this side of the mountain the relief was almost twice as much and the slopes of the peak looked a bit intimidating.

Beginning just to the south of the large, nearly vertical face that dominates the west side of the peak, we began scrambling up a steep but readily climbable couloir, where the smooth but fairly solid marble offered a reasonable route. Crazy-looking dikes protruded out of the marble walls, and a few small creeks cascaded in wispy waterfalls down the sides of the mountain. From our aspect and angle, the Matterhorn appeared to have numerous sharp summit pinnacles, which were absolutely brilliant white against the blue sky of that autumn day. After 3000 feet of steep but technically easy climbing, we anxiously anticipated reaching the crest of the ridge, where we could then look out over the Ice Lake cirque basin and out towards the east. With the summit of the Matterhorn just a few hundred vertical feet to the north, we crested the ridge.

What a view! At this elevation, Hurricane Creek was now just a tiny meandering streak of dark blue winding among scattered trees and open meadows, set

Figure 28. The truly massive west face of the Matterhorn from the floor of the Hurricane Creek valley.

in a stupendously deep valley bounded by the Matterhorn-Sacajawea crest on our side and the Hurricane Divide across the way. The rest of the High Wallowas stretched to the west, south, and east, with the bulky summit block of the Matterhorn dominating the view to the north. After a brief, though admittedly disturbing, stretch of roped climbing, we stood atop the peak, gazing 360 degrees across the high crests of the range and the deep valleys between. Aretes, cirques, moraines, tarns, cols, horns, U-shaped valleys, the signs of the ancient Wallowa glaciers were everywhere. After the usual break of water and a snack, we made our way back down the mountain to the valley below, this time taking a route between the Matterhorn and Sacajawea. Though a bit hesitant at first, peering down the smooth gray walls dropping 3500 feet down to the valley floor, we found the route agreeable, the slope never getting steep enough to induce too much fear. After packing up camp, we made our way back down the Hurricane valley, and though tired, cold, and hungry, we didn't fail to notice the rich golden foliage of the larch, the last light atop the crests above us, and a thought that commonly enters one's mind when returning to the "civilized" world after such a trip, "That was definitely a worthwhile way to spend four days on this planet."

Figure 29. Horn, composed of granodiorite of the Wallowa Batholith, rising above the placid waters of Traverse Lake in the southern Wallowas.

Another glacial feature of the range is **erratics**. Erratics are boulders, often quite large, which are carried great distances by rivers of ice, then deposited on the ground as the glaciers melt away. Erratics are especially obvious when the rock type of the erratic is different than the rocks of the surrounding area and when these large boulders are perched thousands of feet above the valley floor. On Marble Mountain in the eastern Wallowas, one can see large granodiorite boulders sitting atop marble at an elevation of 7000 feet. These are erratics, which were carried by glaciers from the granitic central parts of the range to the west and then dropped high on the sides of the mountain.

On a bright sunny day, the bedrock in some areas shines so brightly it appears to be as reflective as the many high country lakes. This shine is a result of an erosion feature of glaciers termed **glacial polish**. Encased in glacial ice, sand and silt acts as sandpaper scouring and polishing the crystalline rock, producing a reflective, smooth

Figure 30. The distinctive U-shaped upper West Fork Wallowa River valley. Cusick Mountain is the horn in the distance at the head of the valley.

surface. These surfaces of glacier polish are noticeable in some areas of the range underlain by the granodiorite of the Wallowa Batholith, though over time they will lose their luster as weathering of the rock continues.

Glacial striations form as rocks encased in the ice scour and abrade the underlying rock, forming lines or striae. These striations can be seen throughout the range, but are most developed in granodiorite bedrock. They are especially noticeable in the Lakes Basin and near Ice Lake.

Periglacial Features

In addition to glacial landforms, periglacial features also occur in the alpine areas of the Wallowas. Some peaks have rock glaciers, moving rock flows that resemble ice glaciers but are piles of rock often cored by ice below. One such feature can be seen beneath Krag Peak in the southern range. Solifluction lobes are also flow-like piles of rock but form from diurnal temperature fluctuations. Temperatures at these elevations rise above and drop below freezing daily during the warmer months of the year.   This swelling and shrinking of water within the soil, combined with gravity pull downslope, can lead to imperceptible flow of unconsolidated rock debris.   A distinct lobe shape with a prominent scarp of a few feet or more in front may form as the rocks and soil creep downslope. **Alpine subnival boulder pavements** occur in the range as well.   These are flat cobblestone-like mosaics of rock. They appear to be a result of freeze-thaw activity occurring during the late summer and fall.   As this activity occurs, snows may begin to accumulate on top of the rocks surface, "squishing" them down into the unfrozen soil below, and forming a tight mosaic of flat cobbles.   Both solifluction lobes and alpine subnival boulder pavements can be seen above Ice Lake beneath the Matterhorn in the northern Wallowas.   These features appear to be more common in areas underlain by the Hurwal Formation, perhaps because of the layered nature of the rock and its higher clay and silt content.

FLORA

The Forests

Beginning as open stands of ponderosa pine and extending upward in elevation to scattered groves of subalpine fir and whitebark pine, a predominantly coniferous forest covers much of the Wallowa Mountains. The extensive forests of the Wallowas, and those of the other ranges of the Blues, have a distinctly Rocky Mountain flavor and include species that are uncommon in or absent from the forests of western Oregon. Western larch and grand fir are major components of these east-side forests, and aspen and lodgepole pine become more abundant in the colder, drier climate on this side of the Cascade Range. Though the trees of the Blue Mountain region do not approach the enormity of those growing in the maritime climate of western Oregon, where Douglas-fir grow to heights of 300 feet or more, many large trees can be seen in some areas, especially in the well watered mountain valleys of the Wallowas. Majestic three and four-foot diameter ponderosa pine, western larch, Douglas-fir, and grand fir can be seen in certain localities. These giants, and many much larger, once covered thousands of acres in the Blues but most have been logged and today only a few scattered, remnant old-growth stands remain.

Figure 31. Coniferous forest covers much of the Wallowa Mountains at elevations between 4000 and 8000 feet.

Like most of the Rocky Mountain ranges and the isolated mountains of the Great Basin to the south, the Wallowa Mountains have both an upper and lower **timberline**. The timberline is the elevational limit of tree growth. The elevation of timberline depends on local conditions, namely **slope aspect** (the direction a slope faces), precipitation, annual temperature, and soil type. Lower timberline in the Wallowas is somewhere between 3000-4500 feet. Upper timberline occurs at about 8500 feet, but can vary by as much as 1000 feet (timberline on nutrient-poor marble in the Hurricane Creek valley is at about 7500 feet, lower than usual). The most important factors preventing forest cover at these elevational extremes are usually the lack of available water at lower elevations and cold temperatures, high winds, and deep snowpack found at upper elevations. However, between these climatic regimes, the Wallowas support a rich forest, containing a fairly diverse assemblage of mostly conifers.

Figure 32. Open forest of ponderosa pine along East Eagle Creek.

The dominance of evergreen conifers in the forests of the Wallowas and most of the Northwest is likely a result of the seasonal distribution of the region's precipitation. Though many parts of the Northwest are drenched by rain and snow from October through May, June through September is characteristically very dry and sometimes quite hot. Deciduous trees have difficulty growing and competing with evergreen trees in this climate. Their prime photosynthetic season, when water is needed most, includes these driest months of the year. Deciduous trees are much more common east of the Mississippi and in parts of the southern Rockies where significant seasonal rain accompanies the warmer temperatures of summer. In contrast to deciduous species, the evergreen conifers of the Northwest coastal and montane forests are able to photosynthesize and grow during the cooler, wetter months of fall and spring (and sometimes even winter) when deciduous broadleaf trees have lost or have yet to grow their leaves. The evergreen needles of conifers give them a distinct advantage over broadleaf trees in this climatic pattern. This enables conifers to dominate most areas suitable for tree growth throughout much of the Northwest and in many areas of the Northern Rocky Mountains. Despite this climatic pattern, western larch, a deciduous conifer, is common at middle elevations in the Blue Mountain region.

The **biogeography** of a few of the area's conifer species is notable. Some of the westernmost stands of limber pine and the westernmost Rocky Mountain junipers occur in the Wallowas. These are common conifers of the Rockies to the east, but here they reach their western extension. On the opposite side of the spectrum, mountain hemlock, a common subalpine tree of the Cascades to the west, grows in a few localities in the western and central Wallowas. This species is at its eastern limit here, generally preferring the cloudier and wetter conditions so prevalent in much of the western part of the state. These outlier species add diversity and interest to the forests of the range.

Forest Trees

<u>Conifers</u>

The inland forests of the Wallowa Mountains are dominated by coniferous, or cone-bearing, trees. Many of the ranges long valleys are thickly forested, forming a deep green blanket below the barren alpine peaks and above the rolling grass and shrublands at the base of the range. The forests of the range include over a dozen species of conifers.

These include, generally as one moves from the lowest to the highest elevations: western juniper, Rocky Mountain juniper, ponderosa pine, Rocky Mountain Douglas-fir, western larch, Pacific yew, lodgepole pine, grand fir, western white pine, Engelmann spruce, subalpine fir, mountain hemlock, limber pine, and whitebark pine. Some of these trees are found in only a few scattered localities, while others are common throughout the Blue Mountain region.

A Few Tips in Identifying the Wallowa Conifers

1. Are the needles singular, in bundles of two or more, or does the tree have scales? (if they are singular, it is a fir, spruce, or Douglas-fir, if they are in bundles it is a pine or larch, if they are scales, it is a juniper)
2. Where is the tree? (if you see a pine at 7000 feet, it probably is not a ponderosa pine, as this pine is found at much lower elevations in this region)
3. What does the bark look like? (is it reddish, flaky, thin or thick, furrowed, etc.)
4. What do the cones look like? (true firs have upright cones which disintegrate on the tree, Douglas-fir has distinctive "tongues" on its cones, limber pine has large cones, etc.)

Western Juniper and Rocky Mountain Juniper

Small stands of western juniper occur in some areas along the forest/steppe or forest/grassland ecotones at the base of the Wallowas (an **ecotone** is a transitional area between two major plant communities). This scaled conifer grows in the hottest and driest areas where other conifers cannot survive. Though scattered juniper trees grow near the range, they do not form open woodland savannas as they do at the foot of some other Blue Mountain ranges, particularly the Ochoco, Aldrich, and Strawberry Ranges.

Figure 33. Western Juniper

The West Fork Wallowa River valley is home to a few Rocky Mountain junipers. These are western outliers of a species much more common to the east in the main Rocky Mountain belt. This species occurs no where else in Oregon except Wallowa county and is at the western end of its geographic limit.

Ponderosa Pine

Beautiful stands of ponderosa pine form the lowest belt of continuous forest at the base of the Wallowa Mountains. The transition

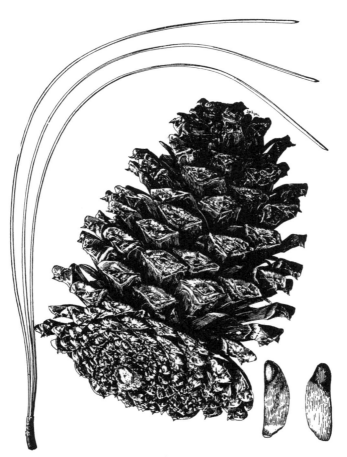

Figure 34. Ponderosa Pine

from grassland, sagebrush steppe, or in some cases open western juniper savanna can be quite abrupt and usually occurs at about 4000 feet along the southern range and 4600 to 4800 feet along the north and northeastern side of the mountains. Water availability is the most prominent factor in distribution of the pine forest. Fingers of ponderosa pine can extend down to 3200 feet along moist drainages and cool, north-facing slopes, and up to 6000 feet on warmer, drier southwest-facing slopes. At higher elevations frost damage begins to severely stunt the tree's growth. Few other conifers can live in the dry, often hot, conditions where ponderosa pine thrives. This drought tolerant species can form lovely, open, park-like forests at the lower timberline of the Wallowas. The tree's thick red bark, long bushy needles, and great height make it one of the more beautiful trees of the West.

Ponderosa pine is well adapted to frequent fires and depends on fire to eliminate competition from shrubs or more shade-tolerant conifers such as Douglas-fir. The needles of the ponderosa contain flammable resins that actually encourage frequent fires. These reoccurring fires burn the highly flammable needle litter on the forest floor, killing young saplings of pine or other species that may be competing with the older trees. The older trees have deep, reddish-orange bark, sometimes 6 inches thick on larger trees, which protects the sensitive tissue of the inner tree from these common low-intensity ground fires. As the trees become older their lower limbs die off, preventing fires from reaching their crown. Old-growth ponderosa pines may have 20 to 30 feet of clear trunk before their first lower limbs appear.

Douglas-Fir

Though ponderosa pine can form pure stands it is often accompanied by Rocky Mountain Douglas-fir throughout much of its habitat in the lower montane forest. This species variant found east of the Cascades and in the Rockies does not reach the immense size of its coastal counterpart, which is among the largest trees in the world. However, on favorable sites the tree can become quite large reaching 4 feet or more in diameter at breast height. Large Douglas-fir often grow on open, well-watered south-facing slopes in the High Wallowas from 5500 to about 6500 feet. Though named Douglas-fir, the tree is not actually a true fir (*Abies*), hence the hyphen in its name. The most obvious indication of a true fir is upright cones at the top of the crown which disintegrate on the tree, a feature the Douglas-fir does not have.

The Douglas-fir can tolerate a wide range of ecological conditions, with the exception of extreme cold, and subsequently can be

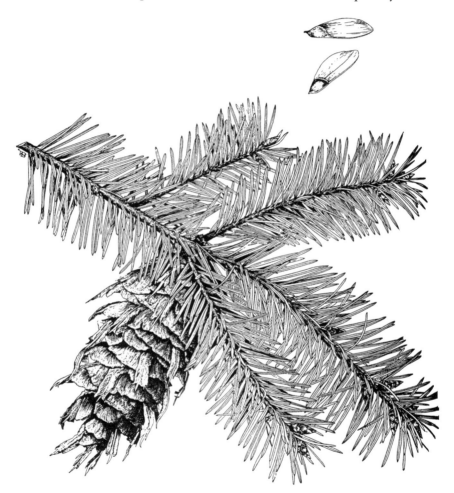

Figure 35. Douglas-Fir

found at many different elevations and exposures. The tree tolerates shade much better than its lower slope counterparts (i.e. ponderosa pine) and is more drought-tolerant than any of its upper elevation neighbors (i.e. Englemann spruce or grand fir). Douglas-fir is common from 4500 to 5500 feet, as precipitation increases slightly and temperatures cool.

Western Larch

Western larch joins Douglas-fir and ponderosa pine above about 4500 feet in elevation, forming a relatively open mixed-conifer forest. This distinctively beautiful tree, with its lace-like, delicate foliage, can dominate recently disturbed sites but is more often found scattered among other conifers. The tree extends from the upper ponderosa pine belt up into the lower edge of the subalpine forest to elevations near 7000 feet. In eastern Oregon western larch is commonly called tamarack after the tamarack of the northeastern United States, but it is in fact a different tree. The larch's light green foliage, open wispy crown, and long, straight, branchless trunk distinguish it from other conifers. The tree is a deciduous conifer, interesting in that it not only bears cones like other conifers but also sheds its leaves, in this case needles, every fall. The needles of the tree turn a rich yellow-gold in autumn adding brilliant color to the otherwise deep green forests.

Western larch is a fire pioneer, invading burned-over sites quickly and effectively by growing much faster than its competition, thus monopolizing available nutrients, sunshine, and water. However, the tree is highly intolerant of shade, and other more shade tolerant conifers can eventually grow in the understory of established larch, forming mixed-conifer stands.

Large, old western larch are quite fire-resistant. The lower limbs of older larch are often tens of feet off of the ground, preventing a "fire ladder" to the crown. The thick, reddish-tan bark of the trunk protects the tree's inner cambium layers from being damaged by the heat of low to moderate-intensity fires.

Because the tree is at its southern geographical limit in this region, larch is not often seen growing on south-facing slopes in the

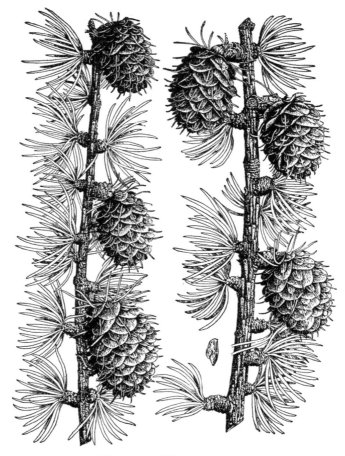

Figure 36. Western Larch

Blue Mountains except where water is abundant. It prefers the cooler, moister conditions found on north-facing slopes. The tree can grow to considerable size, towering over smaller species such as subalpine fir and Engelmann spruce at higher elevations. On favorable sites in the Wallowas, many large western larch reach diameters of approximately 6 feet, their crowns reaching a height of nearly 150 feet. In autumn these older larches are truly impressive, their crowns of brilliant yellow foliage rising well above the surrounding forest.

Figure 37. Aspen and western larch along the South Fork Imnaha River.

Western larch is the only one of 10 larch species known world-wide that is not confined to subalpine and alpine areas or high-latitude boreal environments. North of the Wallowas in central Washington and eastward to Glacier National Park a closely related larch, the subalpine larch, grows at the extreme upper limit of timberline. In some areas western and subalpine larch can be seen growing near one another and even hybridizing, but generally their habitats do not overlap.

There are many interesting and beautiful trees growing throughout the numerous mountain ranges of the West. The mountain hemlock of the high western Cascades, the giant sequoia of the Sierra Nevada, the quaking aspen of the San Juan Mountains in Colorado, these trees seem exceptional in their form and beauty and as a distinguishing characteristic of these majestic mountain areas. Of the trees of the Wallowas, perhaps none is as interesting as the western larch (Larix occidentalis). The larch is relatively common at middle elevations (5000 to 7000 feet) throughout the range, and is notable botanically in that it is a deciduous conifer. The tree's preferred habitat and morpholo-

gy give it a distinctively northern or "boreal" feel (its range actually extends into the Rockies of southern Canada but not much further), with its slender crown sparsely covered in light green foliage in the spring and summer, brilliantly colored gold for several weeks in the fall, and subdued but revealing its delicate, naked branches during the cold and cloudy days of winter.

One of the great joys of visiting the Wallowas in the fall, in addition to the often sunny days, crisp, clear nights, and an occasional early-season snowstorm, is the western larch's spectacular display of autumn gold. Usually beginning in early October at higher elevations, the short needles of the tree's crown begin to turn a greenish yellow. Over time the needles turn a radiant yellow and then deep gold before falling to the forest floor. The larch does not usually form pure stands, and for a short time each October the predominantly deep green coniferous forests of the Wallowa high country are enlivened with splashes of luminescent gold. The combination of frosty meadows, scattered gold larch, deep blue skies, and sharp, snow-dusted peaks makes autumn an excellent time to visit the high country of the Wallowas, assuming one can survive the often frigid nights!

Lodgepole Pine

Lodgepole pine, a slender two-needle pine, begins to appear around 5000 feet in elevation. Lodgepole pine often inhabits areas of marginal soil and moisture conditions and can form pure, dense stands in areas disturbed by fire. In the Wallowas, lodgepole pine can be seen growing in exceptionally wet areas at higher elevations and in cold pockets where frost is frequent, as other conifers are far more sensitive to growing-season frosts than this adaptable pine. Lodgepole is an aggressive fire pioneer and competes with western larch and in some cases quaking aspen in establishing forest cover on burned over areas. It is quickly invading many of the recent burns in the range, notably the extensive Canal burn of 1988 on the eastern side of the mountains. The tree is able to produce serotinous cones. These open when subjected to the heat of fire, dispersing seeds on freshly burned areas to accelerate the pine's invasion of an area. Extensive "dog-hair thickets" can be common, where the pines are so tightly spaced and competing so heavily with one another for nutrients and water that after 20 or 30 years many may be only a couple of inches thick and a few feet tall!

Figure 38. Lodgepole Pine

Pacific Yew

The Pacific yew is found in the Minam River valley of the Wallowas, in some drainages north of Enterprise, and in scattered localities throughout the Blues. This small, shade-loving tree is quite common in some parts of the far northern Blues, where a stronger maritime influence (a result of a break in the Cascade crest through the Columbia River Gorge) results in a more humid climate than is found farther south. The Pacific yew prefers this climate, and thus is much more common in the Coast, Cascade, and Siskiyou Mountains of western Oregon, but even there it is not an especially abundant species. The species made the news in the 1980s after scientists discovered that a

Figure 39. Grand Fir

resin in the tree's bark, taxol, is useful in treating lung, breast, and ovarian cancer in humans.

Grand Fir

The symmetrical crown of the grand fir dominates mature forests in the Wallowas above 5000 feet. This tree is commonly called "white fir" by those living in the area due to the white stripes on the underside of the tree's needles. Grand fir prefers the wetter conditions found at middle elevations but generally grows below the main subalpine belt. The forest types where grand fir is dominant are the most extensive in the Blue Mountain region. As a result of fire suppression and logging of more valuable trees such as western larch and ponderosa pine, the fir is increasingly common in the area's forests. The tree prefers moist habitats, and is abundant in the more protected areas along the valley walls of the Wallowas and the other ranges of the Blues. Grand fir can attain heights of more than 120 feet and diameters of 4 feet or more at breast height on favorable sites. A shady grove of these big firs is a welcoming spot on warm summer days in the range.

Grand fir has dark green, flat-lying needles, whitish gray bark, and stout, horizontal branches. It is very tolerant of shade and can be seen growing in the understory of many ponderosa pine, western larch, and Douglas-fir stands. The tree may eventually take over these stands if fire or other disturbances fail to open up the canopy for the other species. Though grand fir can be seen scattered throughout the mountain forests of much of western Oregon, it is only on the eastern side of the state where it becomes a dominant species of the forest. It is closely related to white fir, a species commonly seen in the Sierra Nevada and the southern end of the Cascade Range in Oregon as well as the southern Rockies. Hybrid forms are common in a transitional area stretching from the southern Oregon Cascades up into the ranges of the Blue Mountains.

Western White Pine

Though this pine is uncommon in the Wallowas, it can be found scattered about in other parts of the Blue Mountains, mostly on the Umatilla National Forest. The tree grows throughout much of the Northwest, but west of Idaho it is usually only a minor component of the forest. It is a five-needle pine with slender, flexible, whitish-blue needles. The crown of older trees is quite distinctive with large sprawling branches extending upward off the top of the tree. Often dangling from these limbs are very large greenish-colored cones.

Many stands of western white pine, particularly in northern Idaho, have been decimated by the introduced white pine blister rust. Silviculturilists have been cross-breeding the few naturally resistant

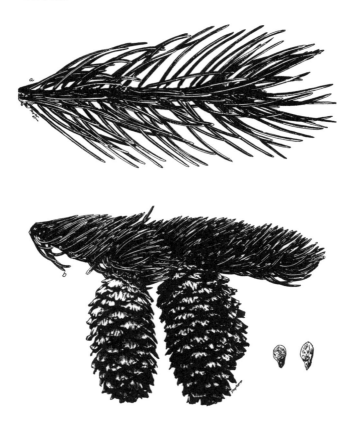

Figure 40. Englemann Spruce

trees in hopes of replanting young pines that are resistant to the fatal fungus.

Engelmann Spruce

In the subalpine forest and at the upper limits of the montane forest, generally above 6000 feet, Engelmann spruce can be seen growing among other Wallowa conifers. The tree has several adaptations to enable it to live in the cold, wet, and windy conditions so characteristic of higher elevations. It is very frost resistant, and can survive temperatures as low as -70°F. Because the spruce has brittle branches and a shallow root system, it grows in tightly packed stands to prevent wind damage to its somewhat fragile frame. The tree prefers cool, wet areas and is often the dominant tree along streams and in shady, moist areas of the high basins. It most often grows at elevations from 5500 to 7500 feet, but extends to lower elevations along streams and rivers. Engelmann spruce is widespread in the Rocky Mountains, and though it is common in the Wallowas, it does not generally dominate the highest forests as it often does farther east. It is most easily recognized by its prickly, stiff needles and often its abundance of reddish brown cones near the top of its crown.

Subalpine Fir

Subalpine fir forms large stands at elevations from 6000 to 7500 feet in the Wallowas and is the most common subalpine tree. To shed heavy winter snows, the subalpine fir has an attractive, slender, pointed crown, which   prevents any significant build-up of snow which could break its very stiff and brittle branches. Beautiful small groves of these trees can be seen in the many parklike areas at the upper limit of the subalpine forest. The elegant, sharp silhouette of the tree is especially noticeable when viewed at a distance, across one of the ranges deep valleys.

Subalpine fir can tolerate a wide range of moisture conditions. It grows in areas receiving as much as 150 inches of annual precipitation (in the Olympic Mountains of western Washington) and as little as 25 inches. Though the cool and moist habitat of the tree retards most fires, when conditions permit fire may burn large areas of fir forest, as the tree is not well adapted to fire. The lack of frequent fires in the tree's habitat has inhibited the fir from developing fire-resistant qualities like many of its downslope counterparts. Unlike most other conifers of the region, it often has limbs growing all the way to the ground, an easy target for even a low-intensity ground fire. In addition, the fir's bark is very thin and contains flammable resins. Under certain conditions what may start as a minor fire in a fir-dominated forest can quickly become a stand-replacing crown fire.

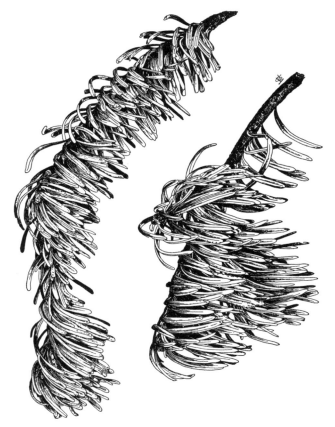

Figure 41. Subalpine Fir

Mountain Hemlock

The mountain hemlock, which commonly dominates the subalpine and timberline environments of the Cascade Range, can also be found scattered throughout the Wallowas at higher elevations mostly in the western part of the range. This conifer requires abundant summer moisture and is confined to exceptionally wet and cool sites. Mountain hemlock is not common on the east side of the Cascade divide presumably because of the lower snowfall and colder temperatures encountered in this region. The tree prefers the milder weather

Figure 42. Mountian Hemlock

and heavier snows of the maritime ranges to the west. However, unlike other ranges of the Blues, parts of the Wallowas are wet enough to provide favorable habitat for the tree. A stand of mountain hemlock can be seen in a USFS Research Natural Area on the far northwestern flank of the Wallowas. Here a nearly pure stand inhabits a moist, north-facing subalpine basin. The tree occurs as far east as the Lostine River canyon of the northern range, and can be seen in a few spots along the East Fork Lostine River trail.

Whitebark Pine
At the upper limit of the subalpine forest near timberline wind and cold prevent establishment of most tree species. Here the whitebark pine makes a home in the thin, poor soil and cold climate characteristic of these upper elevation areas. The sprawling open crown of this pine is easily distinguished from the slender, pointed crown of its frequent associate subalpine fir. The whitebark pine has five-needles to a bundle, and its foliage is characteristically a yellowish-green color.

Figure 43. Mountian hemlock (center) and subalpine fir along the East Fork Lostine River trail.

Whitebark pine is often dwarfed at its upper limit, taking on a picturesque, twisted, wind-beaten form. Some of these flagged trees in exposed areas may actually live in relatively dry habitat despite the abundance of precipitation. High winds scour the surface preventing a significant build-up of snow, while also increasing evaporation leaving the trees susceptible to desiccation. Whitebark pine is especially common on drier, south-facing slopes of the Wallowas above 7000 feet but can be found in fairly moist areas of the subalpine forest as well. The tree extends in a stunted form called krummholz to over 9000 feet on some of the higher peaks in the range.

A mutually beneficial, **symbiotic** relationship exists between this tree and a common bird of the high country, the Clark's nutcracker. The nuts of the pine are a major source of food for the bird, and the nutcracker often caches large quantities of these pine nuts in the ground for later retrieval. However, the birds rarely eat all of the

Figure 44. Whitebark Pine

nuts they bury. As a result, if soil conditions and local climate are favorable, a group of young pines may spring up from a bird's abandoned cache. The bird is an excellent seed distributor for the pine, while the pine is an excellent source of food for the bird.

Limber Pine

The limber pine, a five-needle pine closely related to the white-bark pine, also inhabits the Wallowas. The range is one of only two places in Oregon where one can see the limber pine, which is much more common to the east in the Rockies. Stands of limber pine grow on a calcareous substrate at 7500 feet in the Hurricane Creek valley of the Wallowas and also on drier sites in the Strawberry Range. Named for its supple branches, which can be tied into a knot without breaking, the tree can sometimes be distinguished from the very similar whitebark pine by its larger cones. The flexible nature of the trees' limbs prevents damage from winter snows and strong winds.

Ecological Tolerance of the Wallowa Conifers

The above-mentioned conifers grow in a variety of habitats and elevations largely based on their tolerance or intolerance for certain ecological factors. Ponderosa pine, for instance, grows at lower elevations for a number of reasons, among them: a) it is the area's most drought tolerant species, so it can grow in areas receiving the least precipitation, b) it is more intolerant of frost, and thus grows where temperatures are warmer, c) it is extremely fire resistant, and can outcompete other conifers where fire is typically frequent, such as the dry and warm lower limits of the Wallowa forests.

The characteristics of a tree are tied directly to its tolerance for certain environmental factors, as the trees have evolved and adapted for thousands of years into their current forms. Western larch, because of its low shade tolerance, grows rapidly as a sapling, surpassing other trees in height and thus securing some sunshine to drive the photosynthetic process. Ponderosa pine, with its deep juvenile tap root, has the highest drought tolerance of the major Wallowa conifers, living in the warmest and driest areas. These are a few examples of the adaptive process these trees have undergone to not only compete with other trees but also to survive among different climatic and soil conditions.

Plate 1. Sacajawea, the highest peak in the Wallowas, as viewed from the Hurricane Creek valley. The mountain is composed of massive walls of Martin Bridge Formation.

Plate 2. Sunlight filters onto a meadow along the East Fork Lostine River through a forest of subalpine fir and lodgepole pine.

Plate 3. Sunset reflections on Olive Lake.

Plate 4. Eagle Cap rises above Mirror Lake in the beautiful Lakes Basin, the most popular area in the Wallowa high country.

Plate 5. The eastern High Wallowas from near Tenderfoot Pass. Marble Mountain is the prominent peak on the left with Red Mountain just visible above the ridge on the right.

Plate 6. Early morning light along Bear Creek in the northwestern Wallowas.

Plate 7. Autumn in the high country along Eagle Creek.

Plate 8. Sunlit western larch in fall foliage.

Plate 9. Beautiful Wallowa Lake in winter. Note the large glacial moraines bounding the lake on either side.

Plate 10. The south side of Cusick Mountain from the South Fork Imnaha River. Note the reddish-brown dikes of Columbia River Basalt cutting across the face of the peak.

Plate 11. July brings gorgeous wildflower displays to the high country.

Plate 12. Sunset illuminates a distant thunderhead in soft evening light.

Plate 13. Eagle Cap and the headwaters of the East Fork Lostine River.

Plate 14. Large cottonwoods shade a grassy park along East Eagle Creek.

Plate 15. The northeastern face of the Matterhorn. A small icefield and a recent moraine occupy the cirque just below the shear marble walls of the peak.

Plate 16. Krag Peak rises nearly 4500 feet above the floor of the dramatic East Eagle Creek valley in the southern Wallowas.

Plate 17. A spectacular view of the High Wallowas from Hawkins Pass.

Plate 18. Forest of ponderosa pine in winter.

Plate 19. Colorful Jackson Peak above the headwaters of East Eagle Creek.

Plate 20. View from the slopes of Cusick Mountain toward Red Mountain.

Plate 21. The High Wallowas from ranch near Wallowa Lake.

Plate 22. Peak composed of Columbia River Basalt in the Big Sheep Creek drainage of the eastern Wallowas.

Plate 23. The wild southeast face of the Matterhorn.

Plate 24. The granitic slopes of the south side of Eagle Cap from the East Eagle Creek valley.

Plate 25. A spectacular summer sunset in the High Wallowas.

Plate 26. Moonrise above Glacier Mountain and the peaks above Copper Creek.

Table 5. Conifers of the Wallowa and Blue Mountains

Tree	Elevation Range	Identification
Western Juniper *Juniper occidentalis*	3500 to 4500 feet	Scaled foliage, bluish berry-like "cones", at grassland/forest ecotone
Rocky Mt Juniper *Juniperus scopulorum*	4000 to 4500 feet	Scaled droopy looking foliage, berry-like "cones", fibrous, shredded bark
Ponderosa Pine *Pinus ponderosa*	3000 to 5500 feet	Long needles 4 to 8 inches and 3 in a bundle, dark gray bark turning into reddish tan plates with maturity
Douglas-Fir *Pseudotsuga menziesii*	3500 to 6000 feet	Small blunt, needles 1 inch long all around twigs, brown furrowed bark, distinctive "snake-tongue" bracts on cones
Western Larch *Larix occidentalis*	4200 to 6800 feet	Small light green (gold in autumn) 1" long needles in bundles of 15-30, gray bark turning reddish tan with maturity
Lodgepole Pine *Pinus contorta*	4800 to 7500 feet	Needles 1 to 2 inches long in bundles of two, slender dark trunk, persistent and abundant small cones
Pacific Yew *Taxus brevifolia*	4000 to 5000 feet	½ -1" long flat-lying needles, red "berrys" instead of cones, thin, purple-brown bark, upper branches sprawling and pointed upward
Grand Fir *Abies grandis*	5000 to 6500 feet	Lower needles dark green and flat, two white stripes beneath, light gray bark, stiff horizontal branches, hybridizes with **White Fir** *Abies Concolor*
Western White Pine *Pinus monticola*	5000 to 6500 feet	Needles 2-4 " long in bundles of 5, large cones 6-12" long, needles bluish green, bark cracking into squares with age
Subalpine Fir *Abies lasiocarpa*	5500 to 8500 feet	Needles 1/2 to 1 inch, curving upward, narrow spire-like crown, cones sit right side up at top of tree and disintegrate
Englemann Spruce *Picea englemanni*	5500 to 8000 feet	Short, stiff, pointy needles 1/2 to 1 inch, cones hang downward at top of tree, often droopy look to crown, bark gray, thin, scaly
Mountain Hemlock *Tsuga mertensiana*	6500 to 8000 feet	Needles ½ to ¾ " long, bluish-green with white stomatal stripes, all around twig forming thick, luxuriant look, cones purplish
Limber Pine *Pinus flexilus*	7000 to 7500 feet	Five-needle pine, supple branches, cones 4-6" long
Whitebark Pine *Pinus albicaulis*	7000 to 8500 feet	Needles yellowish-green, 1 to 2 inches long in bundles of 5, open, sprawling crown, cones to 3" long, dense, purplish

Table 6. Ecological Tolerance of Some Wallowa and Blue Mountain Conifers

	LOW	MODERATE	HIGH
Shade Tolerance	WL LP	PP WP DF ES	GF AF
Frost Tolerance	GF PP	WL DF WP AF	ES LP
Drought Tolerance	AF ES	WP GF WL LP	DF PP
Fire Resistance	AF ES	LP GF WP DF	PP WL
Excess Water Tolerance	PP DF	WL GF WP AF	ES LP

WL = Western Larch   DF = Douglas-Fir
LP = Lodgepole Pine   ES = Engelmann Spruce
PP = Ponderosa Pine   GF = Grand Fir
WP = Western White Pine   AF = Subalpine Fir

(adapted from figure in Fiedler and Lloyd, 1995)

Broadleaf Trees and Shrubs

Though conifers dominate most forested areas in the Wallowas, broadleaf trees are also found in certain habitats. They commonly grow along streams, in riparian areas, where water is plentiful throughout the growing season. They can also be found lining meadows, in avalanche-cleared openings, and in especially rocky areas such as talus slopes. These habitats offer a combination of readily available water and, more importantly, an abundance of sunlight as many broadleaf species do not tolerate shade. However, more shade-tolerant species, such as maple, can be common in the understory of some conifer stands.

In the spring the lime green leaves of the area's broadleaf species signal the onset of warmer weather, while in the fall many of the trees and shrubs add a touch of color to the deep green of the predominantly coniferous forests. The cottonwoods and aspens are especially beautiful in the fall as their leaves turn a rich yellow-gold that is truly radiant on a sunny autumn day.

Black Cottonwood

Black cottonwoods grow at lower elevations in the gravelly soil of the many creeks and rivers which drain the high country. These trees are often large, surpassing 100 feet in height on favorable sites. Black cottonwoods occur mostly below 5500 feet, extending to lower elevations along the moist bottoms of major drainages. They line the rivers and irrigation canals of the Wallowa Valley as well as the streams running down the south side of

Figure 45. Black Cottonwood

the range into the sagebrush steppe of the Powder River valley.

The large, spreading crown of the black cottonwood offers important nesting habitat for many large birds including eagles, ospreys, herons, and sometimes even Canada geese. Each tree may have many potential nest sites.

In October, the cottonwood turns a radiant gold, rivaling the closely related quaking aspen in fall color. Large, brilliantly colored cottonwoods are a beautiful sight lining many of the rivers and creeks of the region at middle and lower elevations.

Quaking Aspen

Quaking aspen can be found scattered about the Wallowas on rocky slopes and open, wetter areas at middle and lower elevations. There are some groves in the Wallowa Valley at the foot of the range, but generally aspen is not a particularly common species here or in

Figure 46. Quaking aspen growing in talus field along Eagle Creek.

this part of the country in general. It does not make up a significant part of the montane and subalpine forests as it often does in parts of the central and southern Rocky Mountains.

The quaking aspen's oval, quivering leaves and spotted pale green to cream-colored bark make it fairly easy to identify in the field. The presence of these trees usually indicates that water is very near the surface, at least during the summer months. In the Northwest, aspen commonly grows in areas unfavorable for coniferous competitors, such as talus slopes and particularly wet, open meadows. Aspen stands often have a characteristically lush understory of grasses, as the forest floor is usually clear of snow before the trees' leaves bud in the spring. This enables sunlight to reach the grasses on the forest floor, allowing a headstart on the growing season. Trees of older aspen stands frequently have leaves and branches only on the top one-third of the tree, as the lower branches die off because of the lack of available sunlight. These older stands may have young shade-tolerant conifers in the understory as well, and as aspens are extremely intolerant of shade, over time these stands may be replaced by conifers.

Though aspen is not a fire-resistant species, it recovers quickly following fire and actually relies on frequent fires to open up the forest canopy (increasing available sunlight for growth). An important fire-adaptation is the ability of the tree to sprout new trees from a parent root system. This root system is protected by the overlying soil when low to moderate intensity fires sweep through an area. This adaptation gives the aspen a tremendous advantage over conifers, which must recolonize via seeds. Once aspen has colonized an area, the parent root system is good insurance against both fire and drought, but initial establishment of a grove is difficult.

New colonization of aspen is dependent mostly on availability of water during the tree's sapling stage, and very favorable conditions must exist for aspen to colonize previously uninhabited areas. The tree does not consume an exorbitant amount of water as a mature tree, as it grows in areas receiving as little as 25 inches of precipitation a year, but it is vulnerable to water stress when growing from seed in newly established areas.

Water Birch and Western Paper Birch

The water birch is readily seen throughout eastern Oregon in riparian areas, while the closely related western paper birch grows in a few places along the Minam River in the western Wallowas. The paper birch, a species more prevalent northwest and northeast of the region, is a tree more common to the northern latitudes while the water birch is a shrubby tree

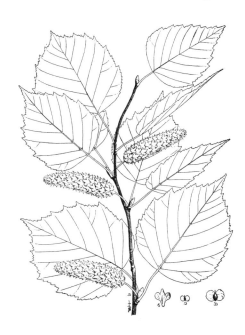

Figure 47. Birch

that often grows in riparian areas of the southwestern United States. Hybridization between these two birches does occur.

Mountain Mahogany

Mountain mahogany grows on dry and rocky slopes in the Wallowas and in other ranges of the Blues. It can grow to tree-like size, but is most often a fairly large shrub. Freshly cut wood is a rich mahogany red color that browns over time. Mountain mahogany grows in some of the harshest

Figure 48. Mountain Mahogany

habitats in the mountains, usually arid, windswept, south-facing slopes.

Willows

Willows are common along watercourses and can be seen along a broad elevational gradient. Some of the subalpine headwater basins of the Wallowas' rivers and creeks, particularly the Bonny Lakes area near Aneroid Mountain, are open areas dominated by grasses, sedges, and thickets of mountain willow.

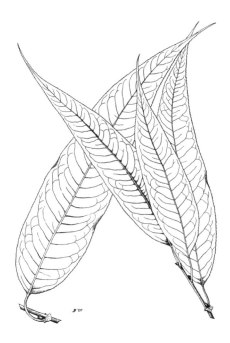

Figure 49. Willow

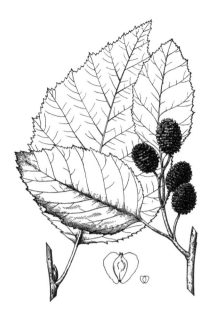

Figure 50. Alder

Figure 51. Serviceberry

Thinleaf and Sitka Alders

Sitka alder is the dark-green shrub covering many ava-lanche-cleared slopes in the high country of the Wallowas. Its leaves are serrated and finely toothed. The thinleaf alder is confined to wetter areas in the range. Pine siskins, chickadees, and other birds feed on the distinctive brown "cones", or female catkins, of both of these shrubs in the winter and early spring when other food sources are scarce.

Serviceberry

This shrub is common in drier areas both in the understory of ponderosa pine and Douglas-fir forests or as a major component of brushy slopes. It's leaf is roundish but toothed only on the end. Serviceberry is a vigorous invader of burned-over areas. Its berries are important diet for many woodland inhabitants, including bears, birds, chipmunks, and other small mammals. Native Americans, and later early frontiersman, made a staple called pemmican from this shrub's berries and dried buffalo meat.

Table 7. Broadleaf trees and shrubs of the Wallowa Mountains

Tree/Shrub	Elevation Range	Identification
Black Cottonwood *Populus trichocarpa*	3000 to 6200 feet	Gray furrowed bark, long (3-6") heart-shaped leaves, common in riparian areas
Quaking Aspen *Populus tremuloides*	3500 to 6500 feet	Small (1-2"long) oval to slight teardrop shaped leaves, whitish green trunk with black marks
Curlleaf Mt. Mahogany *Cercocarpus ledifolus*	3000 to 5000 feet	Tiny evergreen leaves with margins curled under, 2-3 inch long silky streamers attached to fruit, grows on dry, rocky sites
Scouler Willow *Salix scouleriana*	4000 to 6000 feet	Narrow, spatulate leaves 1-3 inches long
Ninebark *Physocarpus malvaceus*	2500 to 5000 feet	Alternate, deciduous, maple-like leaves with 3 palmate lobes
Rocky Mountain Maple *Acer glabrum*	4000 to 6000 feet	Serrated leaf with three main points, 2-4 inches long, forms clump of slender stems, gray bark at maturity, new growth has shiny red bark, "helicopter" seed pods
Big Huckleberry *Vaccinium membrabaceum*	5000 to 7000 feet	Most common shrub in grand fir/subalpine fir forests, edible berries
Thinleaf (Mountain) Alder *Alnus incana*	3500 to 7000 feet	Often grows in pure thickets, leaves double-toothed and not fine like Sitka alder leaves, bent leaf stems
Serviceberry *Amelinchier alnifola*	3000 to 4500 feet	Round, oval leaves toothed *only* at upper end.
Snowbrush *Ceanothus velutinus*	3500 to 5500 feet	Shiny, dark green, evergreen, finely toothed, oval leaves
Wax Currant *Ribes cereum*	2500 to 4000 feet	Very small, indistinctly 3-5 lobed, serrated leaves, waxy upper surface
Swamp Gooseberry *Ribes lacustre*	5000 to 7000 feet	Maple-like leaves (5-lobed), deeply incised and serrate (toothed), spines on bark
Snowberries *Symphoricarpos oreophilus/albus*	3000 to 5000 feet	Opposite, elliptical, deciduous leaves, berries and leaves are poisonous
Sitka Alder *Alnus sinuata*	4000 to 7000 feet	Very fine, sharp teeth on fringes of thin leaves, leaves have varnished look, often grows in dense thickets in moist areas
Pink Mountain-Heath *Phyllodoce empetriformis*	6500 to 8000 feet	Evergreen, linear, needle-like leaf ½ inch long, forms attractive mats at high elevations

Forest Ecology

When walking among the montane forests of the Wallowas, one may notice distinct differences in both dominant tree species and **understory** vegetation as one travels from lower to higher elevations. Differences are also conspicuous between slopes of different bedrock type or aspect, particularly north vs. south-facing slopes. These vegetation patterns are a result of complex interrelationships that the science of **ecology** has sought to understand. Through observation and careful study, ecologists have devised plant community classifications in an attempt to make sense of the variability of forest systems.

Ecologists have defined plant communities based on climax vegetation. The **climax** vegetation of an area is that which will out-compete other species over time and eventually dominate a site for a prolonged period (several hundred years or more) barring any new disturbance. Forests which are considered **disclimax** are thought to be fairly recently disturbed and may include several species which, though they may be abundant at this time, will eventually be excluded as the climax species takes over the site. And though ecologists have learned much about plant interactions and successional patterns, nature is not always so organized and predictable, as evidenced by the difficulties land managers and scientists have faced trying to understand the forests of the Blue and Wallowa Mountains.

Following serious disturbances such as avalanches, high-intensity crown fires, blowdowns, insect infestations, or widespread disease, forests undergo a process of recolonization termed **succession**. In the aforementioned situations, the succession is termed *secondary* succession as the area being colonized was already vegetated previous to the changing disturbance. This differs from *primary* succession, where plants are colonizing a site that was previously unvegetated, such as a talus slope, a recent mudslide, or a recent glacial moraine.

Plants that initially invade sites are considered **pioneer** species. These species recolonize the area and essentially prepare it for the invasion of later successional species. These later **seral** species may occupy the site for several hundred years until finally the climax species take over. Most climax tree species are tolerant of shade and establish themselves in the understory of an early seral stand. They eventually crowd out the less shade-tolerant seral species, forming a new climax forest. Some early seral species, such as western larch and ponderosa pine, are long-lived and can attain great heights. This allows them to remain part of a climax forest for an extended period of time. They simply grow above the cover of the climax species and thus receive enough sunlight to sustain themselves.

Charles Johnson and Steve Simon (1987) did an extensive ecological study of the Wallowa Mountains/Snake River region's plant communities. They defined climax vegetation types based on the dominant tree species and characteristic understory vegetation. Starting with the driest sites sustaining forests and moving upward in elevation to the coldest, wettest sites just below timberline, the climax forest types as defined by these authors include: the Ponderosa Pine Series, the Douglas-Fir Series, the Grand Fir Series, the Subalpine Fir Series, and the Mountain Hemlock Series. Within each of these series are several associations and plant community types based on dominant understory vegetation or in some cases even different dominant tree species.

The Ponderosa Pine Series

At lower elevations on some of the drier, warmer sites, ponderosa pine is the climax tree species. Ponderosa pine climax plant associations can be found from around 3000 feet to about 4800 feet. The most common **understory** components distinguishing communities are common snowberry, spiraea, Idaho fescue, bluebunch wheatgrass, and bitterbrush.

The Douglas-Fir Series

At slightly higher elevations, wetter cooler conditions allow the more shade tolerant Douglas-fir to assume the role of dominant climax species. This series is found mostly from 3500 to nearly 6000 feet. Typical Douglas-fir Series understory species include pinegrass, Rocky Mountain maple, ninebark, spirae, common snowberry, big huckleberry, and mountain snowberry. Ponderosa pine and western larch may also accompany Douglas-fir as long-lived seral components.

The Grand Fir Series

This is the most extensive forest series type in the Wallowas and the other Blue Mountain ranges. It is usually found from 4500 to about 6000 feet. Because of the increase in precipitation and slightly cooler temperatures, this series may include higher-elevation conifer associates as well as lower elevation components sometimes resulting in a varied mixed conifer forest. Typical understories may include queen's cup, Pacific yew, big huckleberry, twinflower, goldthread, Rocky Mountain maple, spirarea, pinegrass, and ninebark. Lodgepole pine dominates many recently disturbed sites in this series and often forms pure thickets after fires or clearcutting. Western larch, Douglas-fir, and ponderosa pine are occasional components in this series. Englemann spruce can also be found here, mostly in riparian habitats.

The Subalpine Fir Series

The subalpine forest of the Wallowas is dominated by the slender, pointed crown of the subalpine fir. This series extends from about 6000 to nearly 8000 feet. Whitebark pine is a fairly common associate of the fir especially on rocky, exposed sites, whereas Englemann spruce can be found in marshy and streamside areas. Lodgepole pine is also prevalent near the lower limits of this series on disturbed sites. In some areas lodgepole pine appears to be the climax tree. At the series' lower limits western larch may become a component of the forest. Typical understory plants include fool's, big, and grouse huckleberries, polemonium, queen's cup, twinflower, twisted stalk, and pinegrass.

The Mountain Hemlock Series

This series is generally restricted to the far western and northwestern Wallowas from elevations of 6000 feet to 7200 feet. The most common understory plants are grouse and big huckleberries.

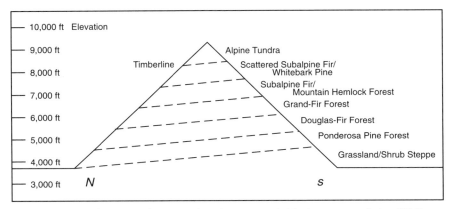

Figure 52. Schematic diagram showing general biotic zones of the Wallowa Mountains. The listed zones are of climax vegetation, though species other than those listed may be common in each zone. For example, western larch may be locally common from the Douglas-fir forests of lower elevations through the grand fir forests and into the subalpine fir forests of higher elevations. Zones occur at lower elevations on the north slopes of the mountains, due to wetter and cooler conditions resulting from less solar radiation.

Fire Ecology and Forest Health

According to some forest and range scientists, the forests of the Wallowas, and the Blue Mountains in general, are among the unhealthiest in the western United States. Years of intensive logging, fire suppression, major insect infestations, and disease outbreaks have caused widespread damage to these forests. Perhaps more than any other single factor, suppression of natural wildfires has wrought ecological havoc on the forests of the Wallowas and the entire Blue Mountain region. Forests are intricate and exceptionally complex natural systems, and there is much we still do not understand. In the dramatic case of the Blues' forests, this has led to tremendous difficulties as scientists and land managers continue to attempt to understand the nature of these east-side forests.

Fire Ecology

Before the institution of fire suppression policies by major land management agencies such as the United States Forest Service and Bureau of Land Management in the early part of this century, natural wildfires were a common phenomenon in many forests of the western United States. These fires would sweep through thousands of acres of forest, commonly only burning the understory of the stands but sometimes paving the way for a new generation of seral tree species such as western larch, lodgepole pine, quaking aspen, or ponderosa pine. In addition to maintaining species heterogeneity, these periodic natural wildfires had numerous other important beneficial effects on forests including:

a) preventing over-stocked sites by killing less vigorous trees and saplings, which in turn reduces competition between the remaining trees
b) renewing soils through nutrient input following burns
c) maintenance of a relatively open canopy resulting in an abundance of grasses and forbs for wildlife forage
d) prevention of widespread insect infestations and disease by favoring healthier trees and killing marginal trees
e) periodic burning of plant or organic litter fuel loads resulting in lower-intensity fires

Today, many forests are over-stocked with young conifer saplings resulting in stands sometimes referred to as "dog-hair thickets". The close proximity of the trees results in stunted growth as they battle one another for the limited available nutrients. The stands often have a relatively closed canopy preventing much understory growth due to the lack of sunshine reaching the forest floor. Often these stands have a tremendous amount of litter, such as dead branches and needles, again restricting available sites for grasses and other understory species. The marginally healthy trees of these dense stands are also very susceptible to diseases, which otherwise may not have been able to spread through an open, more vigorous forest.

A major change in fire intensity, related to changes in forest structure, has been noted following nearly a century of fire suppression. The increased fuel loads, previously limited by recurring low-intensity **groundfires** (in some ponderosa pine forests ground fires are known to have occurred every 2 to 4 years), have resulted in many

Figure 53. The Canal Burn from the floor of the Wallowa Valley. This high intensity fire burned many thousands of acres along the northeastern edge of the High Wallowas. Ferguson Ridge ski area is visible in the center of the photograph.

more catastrophic **crown fires**. A crown fire burns the entire crown of a tree, leaving a desolate landscape of blackened poles in its wake. In contrast, a low-intensity ground fire races along the ground burning grasses, small shrubs, and young trees, but only scarring the trunks of the larger, older trees. Though high-intensity fires may have occurred periodically before wildfire suppression, they are believed to be far more prevalent today because of the available litter to fuel fires and the high-density nature of many tree stands. The high densities of today's forests facilitate the spread of fire via **fire ladders**, formed by layers of branches, small trees, and shrubs that allow flames to climb into the crowns of the trees. Once flames have spread from the ground to the crown of a tree, fire can travel from crown to crown devastating large areas of forest. Older trees that survived ground fires for centuries are now being killed by these high-intensity crown fires.

Fire suppression on the forests of the Blue Mountains, coupled with extensive logging of valuable seral species such as ponderosa pine and western larch, has resulted in a major change in these forests' species composition. The number of seral species such as western larch and ponderosa pine has dramatically declined as the suppression of fire and logging practices have favored the establishment of the more shade-tolerant Douglas-fir and grand fir. Forests that were nearly pure stands of ponderosa pine 100 years ago have reverted to stands of climax Douglas-fir. Slightly wetter areas that may have been dominated by scattered old-growth western larch and ponderosa pine are now thick, mixed-conifer stands dominated by grand fir.

A look at some forest composition statistics recorded in the region over the past century clearly reveal some of the changes brought on by a combination of fire suppression, logging, and grazing of forest lands. According to early Forest Service records, presented in Nancy Langston's excellent book on the historical ecology of the Blue Mountain forests, *Forest Dreams, Forest Nightmares*, in 1906 an estimated 57% of the timber by volume on the Wallowa-Whitman National Forest was ponderosa pine. By 1991 ponderosa pine comprised only 20% of the total volume. As recently as 1938, on the Malheur National Forest in the southern Blues, an estimated 78% of the forests were open pine stands. By 1980 less than half of these were still pine forests. Logging of old-growth ponderosa pine and western larch has significantly affected forest composition throughout the forests of the Blues. In 1906 a Forest Service report estimated open old-growth ponderosa and larch forests covered 800,000 acres on the Malheur National Forest south of the Strawberry Mountains (these forests must have been utterly spectacular). Today less than 1% of these stands remain. By 1991, a survey indicated that on the Wallowa-Whitman National Forest only 18% of the forests were considered mature or old-growth stands. Of this 18%, very few of these were the majestic, open ponderosa pine stands which, less than fifty years ago in some areas, covered thousands of acres on the forest. It is apparent the forests of the Blues have changed dramatically over just the last 100 years, and this change brought on by human practices may be unprecedented in the evolutionary history of these east-side forests.

Forest Health

Insect Infestations

Major insect outbreaks have weakened or killed thousands of trees throughout the Blue Mountain region in the last half of this century. Though insect outbreaks have occurred in the Blue's forests since their development, it is thought that logging practices and fire suppression have led to an increase in severity and possibly in frequency of these often stand-replacing events. Some of the more common damaging insects in the Blues include the pine butterfly, the western spruce budworm, the Douglas-fir tussock moth, the western pine beetle, and the mountain pine beetle. The work of the mountain pine beetle is quite evident in parts of the Blues where one can see large stands of dead and dying lodgepole pine which have been attacked by the insect. Similarly, many stands of both Englemann spruce and Douglas-fir have been ravaged by the western spruce budworm.

The previously noted conversion of many open ponderosa pine forests to thick stands of young climax grand fir has resulted in an increase in insect outbreaks and disease. Grand fir, as compared to the pine, is shorter lived and much more susceptible to disease and insect infestations. In many of today's forests the fir may be living at the edge of its ecological tolerance, as many stands occur in areas barely wet enough to support the trees. When a drought occurs, the trees become highly vulnerable to both damaging insects and disease.

Diseases

Dwarf mistletoe is a common disease infecting many conifer species in the Blue and Wallowa forests, notably ponderosa pine, western larch, Douglas-fir, grand fir, and lodgepole pine. Witchesbrooms, an abnormal proliferation of many small twigs growing on branches of affected trees, often form as a result of this disease. On firs and hemlocks, trunks can swell and crack, leading to further damage by decaying fungi that can cause heart rot of the inner tree.

In many areas of the Wallowas stands of western larch and Douglas-fir have been severely damaged by this disease, leading to widespread mortality.

Indian paint fungus, or brown stringy rot, is a major damaging agent affecting many east-side grand fir stands. It is the most serious heart rot organism of this species, and 25% to 50% gross volume loss has been recorded in old-growth stands. It commonly enters through small branch stubs on suppressed trees. Trees younger than 40 or 50 years old are rarely infected as only limited hartwood has developed during this time. Heart rot and wood rot can severely weaken the structure of infected trees, often resulting in **windthrow** and **windbreak**.

Needle diseases periodically affect several species of conifers in the Blues. These needle diseases are perhaps most conspicuous on western larch. Larch needle blight and larch needlecast both can lead to discoloration (red/orange) and widespread foliage mortality. Despite abundant foliage loss, these needle diseases generally do not cause serious damage to the trees. The larch, being deciduous, can grow new needles rather easily, but reoccurring needle loss may weaken the tree making it more susceptible to other diseases or insect attack. Douglas-fir and the two true firs in the region, subalpine and grand, are also periodically infected by various needle diseases leading to similar discoloration and foliage loss.

White pine blister rust and western gall rust are the most important rusts causing damage to trees in the area. White pine blister rust, introduced earlier this century, has caused more damage than any other conifer disease found in the West. It has destroyed thousands of acres of western white pine throughout the tree's range, especially in Idaho, and also has killed many subalpine stands of whitebark pine. Since the 1920s millions of dollars have been spent trying to eradicate its alternate host, *Ribes*, in hopes of saving some pine stands. The western gall rust is another rust that can damage conifers of the region, especially ponderosa and lodgepole pines, but it has been nowhere near as destructive as the white pine blister rust.

Figure 54. Granitic peaks rise above timberline in the cirque of the East Fork of Elk Creek.

Timberline and Tundra

Alpine Timberline

At the uppermost elevations the continuous forest belt of the Wallowas finally gives way to a treeless region dominated by small alpine plants. This transition from forest to tundra is gradational and is termed the

timberline. Conditions are so severe above timberline that trees are no longer able to survive. Here, temperatures can fall below freezing any night of the year, dessicating winds can exceed 100 miles an hour, and in sheltered areas snow depths can approach 20 feet.

Timberline occurs at different elevations in the Wallowas depending mainly on local precipitation, slope aspect, and **substrate**. It is generally lower in the western and central High Wallowas, as the snowpack here is deeper than on the range's eastern side. Timberline is usually lower on north-facing slopes, compared to those facing south, as these areas receive less solar radiation, resulting in colder temperatures and longer-lasting snows. The prevailing southwesterly winds of the area also deposit large amounts of windblown snow on north and east-facing slopes resulting in a deeper snowpack.

Soil type can also affect the upper limit of tree growth. Mineral-poor soils such as those derived from limestone or serpentine can result in exceptionally low timberlines. The low soil-fertility make it that much harder for a tree to survive in an increasingly difficult climatic regime. Thus trees "give up" at a lower elevation than is typical for the area. The marble and limestone of the Martin Bridge Formation exposed in the High Wallowas has resulted in slightly lower timberlines than would be expected for the area's climate.

Timberline in the range varies from a low of about 7600 feet on limestone near Frazier Lake and in the Hurricane Creek valley to a high of over 9000 feet on the south side of Aneroid Mountain in the eastern Wallowas. Just below true timberline subalpine conifers often revert to ground-hugging, shrub-like mats called **krummholz**. Growing horizontally rather than vertically, the trees are able to escape fierce winds and retain precious heat. The height of the tree is often determined by the depth of the snowpack, as the snow cover serves as a protecting windbreak. Any portion of the tree that attempts to grow above the average snow depth is subject to **dessication** from drying winds and would likely be killed. The growth rate in the harsh climate of timberline is exceedingly slow, and trees hundreds of years old may be less than a foot in diameter.

Though many of the peaks of the High Wallowas barely rise above climatic treeline, recent glaciation, poor soil development, and frequent avalanches have resulted in slow tree colonization of many areas above 7500 feet. Above this elevation, especially in the many deep cirque basins, tree cover is often quite thin and discontinuous giving the range more of an "alpine" feel.

Tundra

Above timberline, small, compact flowering plants grow in a marginal habitat characterized by high winds, frigid temperatures, and heavy snows. These plants growing above timberline often have a growing season between 6 and 8 weeks. In order to survive in this extreme climate several adaptations are characteristic of these alpine plants. They usually grow close to the ground to help conserve available heat and to stay out of the strong winds common at these high elevations.

Figure 55. Alpine tundra above Tenderfoot Pass in the eastern Wallowas.

Shrublands

Just as the Wallowa forests have been divided into series types based on potential climax vegetation, so have the lower-elevation shrublands and grasslands found at the base of the range. Climax and seral shrublands occur at middle and lower elevations along the periphery of the Wallowas and other Blue Mountain ranges. They often occur in ecotonal areas between forests and grasslands and, in the more arid areas of the region, between scablands and wetlands. They are also termed shrub-steppe communities.

Shrub-Steppe Vegetation

A shrub-steppe community composed principally of ninebark and common snowberry is common on more **mesic** (wet) sites on the flanks of the Wallowas. This association can be readily seen in the Grande Ronde valley near Elgin on the western fringe of the range. Shrublands dominated by sagebrush are common throughout much of the Blue Mountain region, and in the Wallowa country most notably on the southern edge of the range in the Powder River Valley. On wetter, cooler sites mountain big sagebrush forms a shrubland with mountain snowberry, elk sedge, and Idaho fescue. This community can be found as high as 6000 feet in the eastern Wallowas. It also extends to lower treeline along the southern fringe of the range in the Powder River valley where it mixes with forests of ponderosa pine and Douglas-fir. At slightly lower elevations low sagebrush forms communities with Idaho fescue and Sandberg's bluegrass. Another species of sagebrush, stiff sagebrush, forms communities with Sandberg's bluegrass on some of the more **xeric** (dry) shrubland sites. On the hottest, driest sites in the deep canyons of the Imnaha and Snake Rivers just east and northeast of the Wallowas smooth sumac, netleaf hackberry, and green-bush form a shrubland with bluebunch wheatgrass.

Grasslands

Extensive grasslands are common throughout the Blue Mountain region especially at lower and middle elevations. These grasslands, or steppe, greatly enhance the biological diversity of the area and are an important component of the east-side landscape from the lowest elevations of the area's canyon country to the subalpine meadows of the High Wallowas.

Drought-tolerant grasses grow in the hot, arid canyon-country of the lower Snake and Imnaha River drainages to elevations as low as 1500 feet. At slightly higher elevations, from about 3000 to nearly 5000 feet, grasslands dominate many south and west-facing slopes and often form a lovely mosaic with pine, larch, and fir forests. At the highest elevations, on deep, well watered soils in the High Wallowas, bunchgrass meadows are common and are a distinct component of the subalpine landscape. Though large open areas dominated by native grasses such as green fescue, Idaho fescue, and bluebunch wheatgrass were once widespread in the region, heavy grazing in the last 150 years and suppression of natural wildfires has led to deterioration and in some cases extirpation of many of these communities.

Green Fescue Series

Subalpine bunchgrass communities dominated by green fescue grow in the cold, moist climate of the High Wallowas. The cooler and wetter climate at these higher elevations allows green fescue to out-compete Idaho fescue, which is often the climax grass at lower elevations. Soils for the green fescue plant association are typically deep, averaging 40 inches, and have a high water holding capacity enabling the grass to grow in what would otherwise be a very harsh environment. The fescue forms a dense sod that helps retain moisture through the summer drought period which at these elevations is generally only about a month long.

Stands in a mid-seral stage are characterized by a codominance between the fescue and spurred lupine as well as a greater component of needlegrasses and sedges (typically Hood's sedge). Late-seral stands may be 65% fescue with less than 1% spurred lupine.

Heavy grazing by domestic sheep earlier this century in the sub-alpine basins and ridgetops of the Wallowas resulted in widespread degradation and successional retrogression of the bunchgrass communities. Areas once covered by a continuous cover of fescue are now

Figure 56. Green Fescue

Figure 57. Rich subalpine grasslands of green fescue once covered parts of the High Wallowas, such as here at the headwaters of the North Fork of the Imnaha River.

dominated by needlegrasses, while others have degraded into an earlier seral stage where lupine dominates over the fescue. Wind and water erosion also accelerated due to the lack of vegetative cover resulting in soil removal in some areas. Restrictions on grazing in the High Wallowas implemented later this century have given some of the communities an opportunity to recover. Perennial plants are recolonizing a few of the most-damaged sites, but many former fescue communities may not return to their pre-grazing conditions for some time.

Idaho Fescue Series

At middle and lower elevations, Idaho fescue, often with bluebunch wheatgrass, is the dominate native bunchgrass. The Idaho fescue-bluebunch wheatgrass association is widespread in the Wallowas and other Blue Mountain ranges and dominates many sites in the surrounding canyonlands. The bunchgrasses usually comprise 50% of the vegetative cover in late seral stands, with forbs and annual grasses making up the rest. Early seral stands of this community are characterized by a bunchgrass cover of only 25%, and other species such as arrowleaf balsamroot, creamy buckwheat, and yarrow may become a significant component. Other common associates of the Idaho fescue-bluebunch wheatgrass association include prairie junegrass, common snowberry, Snake River phlox, elk sedge, and timber oatgrass.

Late seral bunchgrass sites typically have a non-vegetated cover of about 30%, while that of degraded communities may be greater than 60%.

Bluebunch Wheatgrass Series

Bluebunch wheatgrass is the climax bunchgrass on many low elevation sites and south-facing slopes. The grass is more drought-tolerant than either green or Idaho fescue, which are often the dominant species in the cooler wetter microclimates at higher elevations and on north and east-facing slopes.

Sheep and Cattle Grazing

For over one hundred years, domestic sheep and cattle have been grazing the subalpine grasslands of the High Wallowas. Grazing began shortly after Euro-American settlement, about 1880, and quickly increased thereafter as shepherds and stockmen discovered the rich forage of the grasslands of the range. By the mid 1890s several hundred thousand cattle and sheep followed the melting snow to the high summer ranges above 7000 feet, returning to the lowlands following the first significant snows of autumn. During this early period, the forested country of the Wallowas had not yet been designated a national Forest Reserve, like the Cascade forests to the west, and thus grazing in the region was completely unregulated for about a 20 year period. Though this was a relatively short span of time, the widespread effects of this period on native grassland communities can still be seen today.

Initially, the abundant forage of the range's green fescue grasslands was available to graziers on a "first come, first serve" basis. This led to tremendous competition among sheepherders and stockmen,

Figure 58. Idaho Fescue

Figure 59. Bluebunch Wheatgrass

and in turn rapid exploitation of the available forage in the area. Graziers would reach the fragile communities as early in the season as possible with as many animals as possible, often leaving in their wake muddy fields with grasses cropped to the ground. The rich grasslands of Tenderfoot Basin in the eastern range were nearly destroyed by 1900, less than a decade after the onset of grazing in the area. As a result of this time of intense overgrazing, the forage productivity of the mountain grasslands dropped dramatically in just a few years, and sheep and cattle numbers dropped accordingly. The range could not support anywhere near the original numbers set out by early shepherds and stockmen. The number of sheep grazing on the Wallowa-Whitman National Forest decreased from 252,000 in 1906, to 121, 740 just 5 years later, to well below these stocking levels today.

The effects of the intense grazing period of the late 1800s and early 1900s included significant topsoil erosion, gully formation, pedestal formation, a marked decrease (in some areas 100%) in climax green fescue cover, and a loss of herbaceous groundcover. Completely denuded areas, those without any vegetative cover, were not uncommon. Despite the deteriorated condition of the grasslands, overgrazing continued in many areas into the 1940s, as wool production remained an important commodity, supporting the Wallowa sheepmen and thus the local economy of the area.

The effects of early sheep and cattle grazing in the Wallowas are still readily evident today. Many former green fescue grasslands today consist of perennial forbs, needlegrasses, or sedges with only minor representation of fescue, and many recovering areas still have very low percent vegetative cover (<20%). A few areas, closed to grazing for much of the latter half of this century, are beginning to recover through the ongoing process of succession. On the once badly overgrazed Standley allotment in the northwestern Wallowas, the site of one of the first range research studies conducted on National Forest lands (by Dr. Arthur Sampson between 1907 and 1911), it appears, though the historical devastation is still apparent, that the native bunchgrass communities are slowly recovering.

Noxious Weeds

Bunchgrass communities of the Wallowas and the surrounding basins often consist of tufts of native bunchgrasses, such as Idaho fescue, interspersed with a ground-covering crust of lichens and mosses. Intense grazing practices over the years have damaged this crust in many areas, providing an open spot for both native **annuals** and **exotic** species. Though seral native annuals are eventually outcompeted by the bunch-grasses of the region, unfortunately some exotic species are not. The introduction of noxious weeds, which have become well established on these disturbed sites, has dramatically affected the condition of the range and the bunchgrass ecology of the area's native grasslands.

One of the most destructive species introduced to the area is cheatgrass. Presumably imported from central Asia with wheat seed stocks that were being used to plant wheat at the base of the northern Blues, this exotic grass became well established in the region by the 1940s. Cheatgrass has one key evolutionarily derived characteristic that the native bunchgrasses do not; cheatgrass can sprout from seed in pulses over an eight-month period, unlike bunchgrasses that sprout all at once. This trait makes cheatgrass very drought-tolerant. If some seeds wither and die during a long dry spell, another seed bank remains in the soil that can sprout when conditions improve. This competitive advantage over bunchgrasses allowed cheatgrass to invade damaged grassland communities not only in the Wallowa region but throughout the Intermountain West.

Riparian Habitat

Riparian habitat is a special habitat type which spans nearly all elevations of the range. It occurs along a narrow strip adjacent to a river or a stream. This habitat is characterized by abundant water and thus commonly differs from surrounding areas, especially at lower elevations where precipitation is typically less. Here, the local **microclimate** supports different plant and animal species than those found just a few feet away from the riparian corridor. The combination of readily available water and higher species diversity typical of riparian areas make them especially critical to wildlife.

Whereas coniferous trees dominate most forested land throughout the region, broadleaf trees and shrubs such as cottonwood, aspen, alder, and willow commonly dominate riparian areas. These deciduous plants take full advantage of the available moisture along rivers and streams. Riparian habitat is usually associated with perennial water sources, but some intermittent (flow part of the year rather than all year) creeks can also support typical riparian species. The presence of water-loving species in these areas indicates that water is often just below the surface.

Figure 60. Riparian habitat can be seen at nearly all elevations in the Wallowa country.

Wildflowers

Depending on the time of year and the elevation, gorgeous wildflower displays enliven the grasslands, steppe, forests, and tundra of the Wallowa country. The earliest blooms occur in March and April in the warm canyons of the Imnaha and Snake Rivers, with most of the flowers in the Wallowa foothills blooming in May and early June. As spring turns to summer in the high country, lovely wild-flower displays can be seen in the subalpine meadows and grasslands of the High Wallowas, usually peaking in mid to late July.   As the snows recede to the shadiest, coldest corners of the range, summer follows right behind, slowly marching its way up the mountain slopes, turning what were previously cold, wet, and snow-choked meadows into brilliant green blankets, touched with the purples, reds, whites, blues, and yellows of the area's wildflowers.

Wildflowers of the Wallowa Mountains

Western Yarrow
Pearly Everlasting
Prickly Sandwort
Queen's Cup/Beadily
Creamy Buckwheat
Wallowa Lewisia
Linanthastrum
Longleaf Phlox
Starry False
   Solomon's Seal
Cusick's Milkvetch
Heartleaf Arnica
Hoary Balsamroot
Common Camas
Clarkia, Pink Fairies
Showy Aster
Tallcup Lupine

Blue Mountain
   Penstemon
Skunk-Leaved
   Polemonium
California False
   Hellebore
Subalpine Daisy
Yellow Buckwheat
Oregon grape
Cusick's Camas
Forget-me-not
Mullein
Mule's Ears
Kinnikinnick
Arrowleaf Balsamroot
Currant
Snowbrush

Twinflower
Sego Lily
Mountain Arnica
Geranium
Saxifrage
Buttercup
Wallowa Primrose
Larkspur
Silky Lupine
Monkeyflower
Paintbrush
Columbine
Lady Slipper
Cow Parsnip
Mountain Bluebells
Coral Root

For additional information and excellent photographs of wildflowers and other plants of the Wallowas and the surrounding region see Charles Johnson's comprehensive *Common Plants of the Inland Pacific Northwest*, published by the United States Forest Service.

Paleoecology

Though the vegetation we see today in the Wallowas and the other Blue Mountain ranges may seem like it has always been here, studies suggest that dramatic changes in plant distribution have occurred in the area during the last 10,000 years. Since the last major glaciation and throughout the Holocene, vegetation patterns have changed in response to significant climatic fluctuations. Biotic communities that are widespread today may not have existed just a few thousand years ago, and species that today dominate parts of the region may have been minor components of the area's plant communities in the past, or, in some cases, may actually be only recent immigrants to the Wallowa country. Evidence for significant changes in this region's biota has mostly come from the study of pollen preserved in lake sediments throughout the Northwest.

The study of pollen, **palynology**, has taught us a great deal about the dynamic nature of the earth's plant life. Palynologists are able to collect sediment cores from lakes of a region, date intervals in the cores using methods such as radiocarbon dating, and interpret plant abundance based on the pollen grains they find within each dated interval. Macrofossils such as preserved needles are also used to differentiate species.

Though paleoecological studies of the Wallowa region are limited, others undertaken north and south of the area indicate that cold sagebrush steppe dominated most of eastern Oregon and Washington during the Wisconsin glacial period. During this time (from about 25,000 to 12,000 years ago), the climate was apparently too cold and dry to support much coniferous forest. Preserved pollen in lake sediments is dominated by sagebrush and grasses, with evidence of conifers not appearing in some areas which are forested today until perhaps 4000 years ago. Some cores reveal more spruce and birch pollen, again indicating cold, dry conditions during the glacial advances of the Wisconsin period. Beginning about 12,000 years ago conifers began to invade into the steppe communities, only to decline with the onset of the **Altithermal** (a period of warmer and drier conditions during the Holocene from about 6500 to 4500 years ago). During this warmer period, grasslands appear to have been much more extensive. Finally, beginning about 4500 years ago, climatic conditions similar to the present resulted in maximum forest expansion into steppe grasslands. Since this time landscape-scale vegetation patterns on the east side of the Cascade Range, though still quite dynamic locally, have remained relatively stable.

A few limited pollen studies at Twin Lakes in the Wallowas and at Lost Lake to the west have revealed some information about the spatial evolution of the area's plant communities, but much is still not known concerning the region's vegetation history. The Lost Lake core, taken near Dale, contained mountain hemlock pollen indicating the presence of this conifer nearby approximately 3000 years ago. Today, the closest stands of mountain hemlock are 60 miles to the northeast, on the western edge of the Wallowas.

FAUNA

The Wallowa-Whitman National Forest, which includes the Wallowa Mountains, portions of the Elkhorn Range and the Blue Mountains proper, and a segment of Hells Canyon, is home to over 400 different wildlife species. This diversity of species can be attributed to the diverse habitat found throughout the region, from the warm, arid canyonlands of the Snake and Imnaha River drainages up through the rolling montane forests and into the subalpine meadows and alpine tundra atop the High Wallowas. The many lakes of the Wallowas and the numerous streams and rivers draining the higher terrain of the area support 41 different species of fish, while a remarkable 271 species of birds have been recorded on the national forest. Many threatened species still make a home in the wilderness of the High Wallowas and the surrounding canyon country, as the region, despite some development, ecological changes, and habitat loss, still represents a large area of quality wildlife habitat.

Some of the more popular inhabitants of the Wallowa country are the larger mammals or "big-game" animals. These include the native species Rocky Mountain elk, mule deer, whitetail deer, Rocky Mountain bighorn sheep, cougar, and black bear. The majestic Rocky Mountain bighorn sheep found in the range were reintroduced into the area after having been **extirpated** earlier this century. The mountain goat is an introduced inhabitant of the rocky crests of the High Wallowas, though some biologists suggest the animal could be native to the range.

Recent surveys in the area indicate that deer (namely mule deer rather than whitetail deer) and elk populations in the Blues have declined considerably, with record-low calf survival rates in elk herds occurring in Wallowa County. Some wildlife biologists believe that much of this decline is a result of increased **predation**. According to a few recent studies, northeastern Oregon currently has higher bear, cougar, and coyote populations than at any time since 1900. Population fluctuations in nature are common between prey and their predators. As predators such as bear, cougar, and coyote become more numerous, deer and elk populations subsequently decrease as evidenced by current trends seen in the Wallowas and other parts of the Blues.

Wildlife and Wildlife Habitat Types of the Wallowa Mountains

Many wildlife species prefer a particular habitat type, such as a ponderosa pine forest or a mountain stream, while others can live in numerous habitat types ranging from open juniper savannas to sub-alpine meadows. The fauna of the Wallowa Mountains can be most easily discussed and understood by grouping species by their preferred habitat types. The diverse topography of the Wallowa country, with its soaring peaks, lava-capped ridges, and extensive coniferous forests, includes a number of different habitats that are often in close proximity. These habitat types include lower-elevation grasslands and shrub steppe, ponderosa pine forests, mixed conifer forests, subalpine forests, open subalpine and alpine tundra, and, spanning nearly this entire elevational range, riparian areas.

Wildlife of Grasslands and Shrub Steppe
Sweeping lower-elevation grasslands and shrub steppe occur in the region from 2500 up to about 4500 feet. Idaho fescue and blue-

Figure 61. Coyote

bunch wheatgrass are the principal native grasses of much of the area, while most shrub steppe is dominated by sagebrush. Birds and animals living in the open country of this habitat commonly have very good eyesight and/or speed. These characteristics are helpful in both evading predators and, depending on the species, finding prey.

The grasslands to the north of the High Wallowas once supported large populations of Columbian Sharp-Tailed Grouse, particularly Zumwalt Prairie. Habitat loss has led to a major decline in these populations. However, Zumwalt Prairie still does support an interesting array of bird life, in particular an exceptionally high density of buteos and other birds of prey.

Coyote

The resourceful coyote, long a target of federally funded predator control operations including widespread poisoning, still roams the open steppe country and grasslands throughout the Blue Mountain region. In fact, recent surveys suggest the coyote population in northeastern Oregon may be higher today than at any time this century. The coyote population, as well as that of the cougar, may have grown over the course of this century due to the extermination of the wolf in the region. By 1910, wolves had been killed off in the Wallowa country, opening the door for these other predators. The coyote feeds primarily on vertebrates, in this area the Belding's ground squirrel being a major source of food, but it may also eat insects and vegetables. Hunting in packs, coyotes exhibit an acute sense of smell and hearing, detecting prey at great distances (as well as danger). They have incredible endurance and will chase down prey by simply running them into exhaustion.

Pronghorn

Pronghorn once roamed the plains at the foot of the Wallowas but as of just a few years ago they are no longer found near the range. Only recently a herd of pronghorn lived in the Powder River Valley along the southern end of the High Wallowas, but these animals were relocated by local game officials for eating alfalfa. Pronghorn still roam the sagebrush and juniper savannas at lower elevations near the Strawberry Mountains however, on the southern periphery of the Blue Mountain region. Approximately 4000 years ago, it is thought that pronghorn were quite abundant on the plains surrounding the High Wallowas. Today, this graceful animal is common only in the southeastern corner of the state, where broad sagebrush plains cover thousands of acres providing ideal habitat.

Pronghorn prefer open spaces, as their main defense against predators is their speed (approaching 50 mph in short bursts) and their exceptional eyesight, which has been compared to high-powered binoculars. Although able to jump more than 7 meters in one stride, pronghorn are reluctant to jump over objects, and prefer to crawl under or through fences. In the high desert country this can be a problem as there are numerous barbed-wire fences criss-crossing the open plains. Pronghorn are primarily browsers and feed mostly on sagebrush, bitterbrush, and rabbitbrush, although forbs and grasses are occasionally eaten.

Winters on the steppe of eastern Oregon are characterized by bitterly cold temperatures and strong winds. To deal with this harsh climate the pronghorn has through evolution developed an extremely well insulating hide. The animals' coat is made up of many hollow-cored hairs that effectively trap warm air near the body.

Unlike many other hoofed-animals (ungulates) including elk and deer, both pronghorn sexes develop horns, though the males' are typically larger and with a more definite prong. They are true horns composed of fused hairs that form a bony core. They reach their maximum size during the summer.

Pronghorn are gregarious, travelling in mixed herds most of the year except in the spring when the bucks are alone or in small groups. In the fall the bucks collect harems of up to 15 does. The animals breed in August or September and the young are born in May and June.

Figure 62. Swainsons Hawk

Swainsons Hawk

This hawk is typically seen in open steppe and grassland habitats feeding primarily on rodents. It usually nests in isolated trees but sometimes is found nesting in bushes or on cliffs. The bird has a remarkable migration pattern, flying all the way from central Argentina northward to the western United States in the late spring, and returning on its 5000 mile journey in the early fall. Swainsons hawks, as well as ferruginous hawks, were once common in the area but have experienced a sharp decline recently, probably due to habitat destruction and fragmentation both in the Wallowa country and in other regions inhabited by the bird. Swainsons hawks, as well as ferruginous hawks, are today most commonly seen nesting on the prairies just north of the Wallowas, such as Zumwalt Prarie.

White-tailed Jackrabbit

This rabbit prefers open areas such as sagebrush flats and grasslands but can occupy habitats up to subalpine meadows. It feeds primarily on grasses and forbs in the warmer months and leaves and stems of woody plants during the winter. It is nocturnal and can sometimes be seen dashing out in front of one's headlights or at duck or dawn. Once considered common, this rabbit is less so today likely due to alteration of its habitat, namely the disappearance of native grasses.

American Kestrel

The American Kestrel is a tiny falcon most commonly seen in open country, including sagebrush steppe and grasslands. It can be found foraging in high, open meadows in the mountains, but it generally avoids forested country. The falcon's primary prey is insects, including large insects such as grasshoppers.

Black-Billed Magpie

Elegant-looking black and white birds with long, flowing tails, magpies are actually widespread opportunistic scavengers, feeding on road-killed rodents, other bird eggs and nestlings, and sometimes carcasses of large mammals such as livestock or ungulates. They frequent riparian areas with their thick shrubby cover at lower elevations as well as open agricultural lands, such as those of the Wallowa, Powder, and Grande Ronde valleys, and sagebrush steppe. They sometimes are seen at the lower edges of the regions' coniferous forests as well.

Snow Bunting

A winter migrant, this predominantly white sparrow is among the most cold-tolerant of all the small birds in the region. Uttering a nearly constant twitter in flight, the birds frequent open fields and

Figure 63. Black-Billed Magpie

grasslands, and especially prefer snow-free cultivated lands where grain or weed seeds can be found. The nearest breeding areas for the bird are in northern Canada.

Other Common Species of Grasslands and Shrub Steppe

Belding's Ground Squirrel	Horned Lark
Red-Tailed Hawk	Golden Eagle
Brewer's Sparrow	Loggerhead Shrike
Sage Sparrow	Common Raven
Sage Thrasher	Black-Tailed Jackrabbits
Western Meadowlark	Chukar

<u>Wildlife of Ponderosa Pine Forests</u>

This habitat is found from 3500 feet to about 5000 feet in the region. Fairly open stands of ponderosa pine are typical, with bunch-grasses or scattered shrubs comprising the understory. At higher elevations other conifers such as Douglas-fir or western larch may live among the pines in a transitional zone between this habitat type and the mixed conifer forest habitat of slightly higher elevations.

Figure 64. Mule Deer

These forests are beneficial to many species in both summer and winter. Higher pine forests are moist enough to offer green growth for foragers in late summer when lower elevation grasslands have withered. During the winter, elk and deer may browse on ponderosa twigs and buds, while nuts from cones and insects in the bark support species such as the red crossbill when other food is scarce.

Mule Deer

Though mule deer are common throughout the Wallowa region at nearly all elevations, they are commonly seen in ponderosa pine forests. Named after their large, donkey-like ears, these deer browse primarily on leaves, buds, and twigs of a variety of deciduous shrubs found in the region. Studies have shown that their diet includes more than 800 different plant species. During the summer months they graze the succulent green grasses in the subalpine and alpine portions of the High Wallowas. Deer nibble on a variety of low-quality foods, including fir needles and lichen, during the cold winter months when other sources of nutrition are buried beneath a blanket of snow. Their winter survival depends more on fat reserves accumulated during the summer and autumn and the severity of the winter (cold temperatures) than on the quality of winter forage. Mule deer often live in generally rough and rocky terrain and their stiff-legged bouncing gait is well adapted to this habitat.

After enduring the winter together at lower elevations, in the spring some does leave these groups to bear their young, usually from one to three fawns. They spend the summer with the newborn young, migrating to higher areas as the snows of the winter recede. Many bucks spend the warmer months of the year by themselves wandering among the forests and meadows of the High Wallowas. As mating season approaches in November, the bucks join with doe and fawn groups and begin traveling to lower elevations in preparation for the winter. In recent years, Mule Deer populations have declined considerably in northeastern Oregon. This is thought to be a result of increased predation by a growing cougar population.

Raccoon

The intelligent raccoon lives throughout the ranges of the Blue Mountains. It is omnivorous, feeding on insects, small mammals, birds, fish, eggs, fruits, and nuts as well as sweet corn and other domestic vegetable crops. Raccoons are nocturnal but are occasionally seen in the daytime in their most common habitat type; along streams or near ponds. Female raccoons can give birth annually to up to 6 young, with litter size tending to increase with age.

Yellow-Pine Chipmunk

These little chipmunks are most active from March to November eating seeds, bird eggs, flowers, fungi, and bulbs, roots, and buds of various plants. They prefer brushy areas in ponderosa pine and Douglas-fir forests where snowberry, buckbrush, mountain mahogany, and other shrubs offer cover. They have distinctive black and white

Figure 65. Red-Tailed Hawk

stripes on both their back *and* face, unlike the similar but larger golden-mantled ground squirrel.

Red-tailed Hawk

The red-tailed hawk is the most common buteo of the region, nesting in forests and sometimes in open woodlands or on cliffs in steppe areas. The bird favors large cottonwoods and pines for nest sites. The hawk's principal prey is rodents and small rabbits.

Mountain Bluebird

Along with the Stellar's Jay, this bird is the only one found in the region that is predominantly blue. Unlike the jay, the mountain bluebird is a quiet species, with a song that is soft and warbling. It is fairly common from the mountain meadows of the High Wallowas down to the ponderosa pine forests at the base of the peaks. The bird breeds in open woodlands and forest-edge habitats typically where dead snags or rock crevices are available for nesting sites.

Stellar's Jay

A raucous bird, the Stellar's jay frequents the ponderosa pine forests of the region, though they it can be seen in Grand-fir climax forests and in lower more arid country as well. The bird has a nearly uniform deep blue body with a pronounced dark crest. It is the only crested jay in the West. The jay remains active during the winter, feeding on stored food such as pine seeds. It is a common "camp-robber".

Figure 66. Stellar's Jay

Brown Creeper

This well camouflaged little brown bird can sometimes be seen probing the bark of coniferous trees looking for insects. It has a long, narrow, and slightly curved bill to aid in this search for food. It commonly nests in loose bark of mature trees and these nests are difficult to find.

Mountain Chickadee

"Chick-a-dee-dee-dee, chick-a-dee-dee-dee." The call of the mountain chickadee can often be heard in ponderosa pine forests of the range extending upward to mixed-conifer forests at higher elevations. The bird uses woodpecker holes or self-excavated holes in rotted wood for nesting. They can commonly be seen fluttering about the pines, gleaning small insects off of the bark of the pines and other conifers. Their body is a light gray while their head is distinctively black-and-white striped.

Pine Siskin

This small finch is streaked with brown and white but with yellow

Figure 67. Pine Siskin

markings at the base of its tail and on its inner flight feathers. It is commonly seen in groups in conifer stands, feeding primarily on conifer seeds but also on seeds of alders and birches in wetter areas where these broadleaf trees grow. Like many finches, the pine siskin nests in small, loose colonies. The song of the bird is a goldfinch-like warbling.

Northern Flicker

A beautiful, elaborately marked bird, this woodpecker frequents more open areas rather than dense forests, and is unusual among woodpeckers in that it feeds most commonly on the ground, probing the surface for insects such as ants. It nests in trees, however, excavating holes in

Figure 68. Northern Flicker

dead or decaying trees. The bird has a rather bold, series call. The bird's beautiful markings are distinctive, especially the salmon-colored wings in flight.

Flammulated Owl

This small owl, with its series song, *hoop* or *hoop-hoop* at 3 or 4 second intervals, is commonly heard in ponderosa forests at dusk and in the early hours of the evening. It is a migratory owl, wintering in Mexico and Central

Figure 69. Flammulated Owl

America. The owl feeds predominantly on insects such as beetles or grasshoppers, rather than vertebrate pray. The flammulated owl nests in natural tree cavities as well as woodpecker-excavated holes at least 10 feet above the ground.

The full moon had just crested the high peaks to the east, illuminating the forest in a soft lunar light. The wind had died down to nothing, and there was a deep stillness present in the valley. Walking among the pines and aspen, I had been watching the moonrise for a short while, but now decided to head back toward the light and heat of the campfire. Tired after a rather busy day and full from dinner, I sat down in front of the fire and soon began to stare calmly into the flittering orange flames. As I sat motionless transfixed by the heat, quiet, and crackling sparks of wood, out of the corner of my eye I noticed a slight movement. I initially thought it was a rodent looking for the scraps of our dinner, but turning my head slightly to my right I noticed it was much bigger and standing upright. Here only two feet from me also staring contently into the warm flame, seemingly oblivious to me or maybe even deliberately sitting alongside me, was a small flammulated owl!

I slowly turned my head to get a better look when it looked over at me, its deep brown eyes faintly lit by the fire looking directly into mine. We both seemed a bit startled, or perhaps just awkward (I rarely see owls, and certainly had never been approached by one). After several seconds of contemplation, it flew up into a branch not more than a few feet off the ground, and gave me several introductory "hoop-hoops." After another few moments it flew up and into the forest canopy, leaving me sitting wondering "what just happened here?"

Later I walked out into the dark forest and heard the owl calling again nearby. My initial thought was maybe it didn't see or hear me back at the fire, but the way it looked at me and upon further reflection I think that it may have been just a curious visit at the campfire. Whatever the case, there was a look and a communication between me and that little owl that I will long remember.

Dark-eyed Junco

A year-round resident of both ponderosa pine and mixed-conifer forests, these active little birds are quite common at low and middle elevations in the Wallowas. They have a predominantly gray body and dark black head. Their song is a musical trill, and they are readily identified in flight by conspicuous white feathers on their otherwise black tails. A seed eater, in the winter the junco migrates downslope below snowline, continuing to forage for seeds. In the summer it nests on the ground among grasses or sedges.

Other Common Species of Ponderosa Pine Forests

White- and Red-Breasted Nuthatches   Blue Grouse
American Robin   Golden-mantled Ground Squirrel

Wildlife of Mixed-Conifer Forests

Mixed-conifer forests of grand fir, Douglas-fir, western larch, ponderosa pine, and lodgepole pine occur in the Wallowas and other Blue Mountain ranges from 4500 feet to about 6000 feet. These forests are denser than the pine forests found at lower elevations and often have a richer understory of deciduous shrubs and forbs.

Cougar

The cougar, or mountain lion, inhabits the rugged, forested terrain of the Eagle Cap Wilderness as well as the canyonlands on the periphery of the range. Sightings of this elusive cat are becoming more frequent in the region, but generally it is not often seen by humans. Tracks, scrapes, and other signs of the cat may sometimes be seen along trails in the High Wallowas and in the surrounding area. The cougar inhabits mountain ranges throughout Oregon, and

Figure 70. Cougar

with the demise of the wolf is now the major predator of deer and elk. The mountain lion hunts by quietly sneaking up on unsuspecting prey and then quickly pouncing on them. The population density of the mountain lion is tied directly to the number of deer in an area, as the cat's principal prey is mule deer, though elk are commonly preyed upon and even porcupine are periodically eaten as well. Uneaten freshly killed prey is buried, and the cat remains in the general area until it has been consumed. An entire deer can be consumed in just two nights.

Mountain lions may breed at any time during the year. Litters commonly include between two and four kittens. The young remain with their mother from 15 to 22 months, learning necessary survival skills. Mountain lions are solitary, with adults associating with one another only for breeding purposes. Kittens may travel with adult females for some time, but usually without any other adults.

Cougars are highly territorial, maintaining spatial separation between one another thereby assuring that each individual has the necessary resources to survive. If this separation is not maintained, the animals will kill one another. Mountain lions kill large prey with some regularity, usually one deer-sized animal every 6 to 12 days.

Rocky Mountain Elk

The Wallowa-WhitmanNational Forest, which includes the Wallowas, parts of the Elkhorn and Greenhorn Mountains, and areas near the Washington and Idaho borders, has one of the largest free-roaming elk populations of any national forest in the nation. The sub-species found here is known as the Rocky Mountain elk and is different than that found in the Cascade and Coast Ranges to the west, which is termed Roosevelt elk.

The forest/grassland mosaic so common at middle elevations in the northern Blues offers ideal habitat for elk, or wapiti. Depending on the time of year, elk use forested north and east-facing draws either as thermal cover during cold winter nights or as welcome shade during the hot, dry summers. At middle and lower elevations south and west-facing slopes are most often vegetated with bunchgrasses

Figure 71. Elk

rather than trees, and these grasses are important forage for the herds.

As spring arrives and snows recede farther up into the mountains, female elk, or cows, and their newborn calves head up into the higher drainages where lush plant growth provides important feed. Swelling streams are easy obstacles, as elk are strong swimmers. While the cows and calves graze in groups, the bulls generally travel alone or in small bachelor groups during the spring and summer. In the High Wallowas, elk tend to summer in high, partially wooded subalpine basins near the heads of the range's major drainages.

As summer turns to autumn, elk begin to move to lower elevations. Fall is the rutting season and is a time of heightened activity among the bulls. Much energy is used by the males in fighting or bluffing in order to secure groups of cows and calves, called harems. Beginning in early September, the bugling call of the bulls can be heard in the timbered valleys of the Wallowas. During this time much of the backcountry is alive with hunters as well.

The second largest species of the deer family (the moose is the largest), some bull elk grow to be 6 feet tall at shoulder height and weigh as much as 1200 pounds. These stately animals often have impressive multiple-point antlers which are prized by hunters. The males' antlers are usually shed in March and a new pair begins to grow in April. New antler growth is complete by August just in time for the annual rutting season in the fall. Elk winter in the foothills and valleys beneath the high peaks where snowcover is thinner and temperatures are warmer. Most of the elk's winter grounds are in private ownership outside national forest boundaries, sometimes complicating management of the herds. This lower elevation habitat is critical during the long, cold winters so typical of much of eastern Oregon.

Elk have distinct summer and winter coats, which are shed in late summer and spring, respectively. In winter, much of the coat is dark brown with a thick undercoat and both sexes have heavy, dark manes. In summer, the coat is more of a reddish brown and lacks the thick undercoat, giving the animal a sleeker, more muscular appearance.

As mentioned previously, large bull elk can weigh up to 1200 pounds, but usually range from 600 to 800 pounds. Cows typically weigh from 450 to 600 pounds. Despite their size, elk are fast and agile animals, having evolved in an open plains environment. They are able to run 40 mph for short bursts and 30 mph for longer periods, and can jump vertically 8 to 10 feet.

Porcupine

A shy, lumbering inhabitant of the range, the porcupine lives in the forests of the Wallowas feeding primarily on forbs, shrubs, and trees. Porcupines are more abundant here than in the forests west of the Cascades. During the winter, they strip the bark of trees and eat the inner cambium, as little else is available to eat at this time of year. They are generally nocturnal, resting during the day under the cover of thick brush or the canopy of a tree. They move slowly, but are protected by their sharp quills discouraging most would-be predators.

Black Bear

The black bear is numerous throughout the Wallowa and other Blue Mountain ranges. Today this is the only species of bear found in the region, though grizzly bears were once common as well, roaming the deep canyons and forested mountains of the Hells Canyon/Wallowa country. The last grizzly recorded in Oregon was shot and killed in Wallowa County in 1931.

Black bears are shy, secretive animals although possessing considerable curiosity and intelligence. They have poorly developed senses of hearing and sight, but this is compensated by an acute sense of smell.

Black bears hibernate in November as winter begins in earnest. They become torpid and seek caves, hollow logs, and other shelter for their winter sleep. They must put on weight during the warmer months to prepare them for this prolonged winter sleep, which lasts about five months. Bears emerge from their dens as spring slowly arrives in April, feeding largely on green grasses and highly prized carrion that did not survive the winter.

Black bears are omnivorous, feeding on both plants and other animals, and their diet consists of a wide variety of items during the summer and fall months. They use their powerful claws and legs to turn over rocks and rip open logs to feast on insects and small vertebrates. They also prey on spawning fish in mountain streams of the region. Currently in some areas of the Blue Mountains black bears are having a serious impact on the survival of newborn elk calves.

Bears breed in June and July and females give birth to 2-3 young cubs usually in January in their winter dens. Sows give birth every two or three years depending on their health. Cubs emerge from their dens in April and stay with their mother through the first summer and fall, also denning with her their second winter. Though sometimes congregating at feeding sites or travelling as breeding pairs, black bears are normally solitary animals. They can travel great distances (over 100 miles) searching out pockets of food.

Golden-mantled Ground Squirrel
        This is the commonly seen small squirrel of the mountain West. It has distinctive black and white stripes on its back but unlike the chipmunk it has no stripes on its face. Its habitat stretches from juniper savanna to timberline but is most common in open areas in ponderosa pine and mixed-conifer forests.

Blue Grouse
        The chicken-like blue grouse has a fairly long, fanlike tail and white underparts. Its habitat includes middle and upper elevation forests, but it is especially common near aspen groves, where the buds and catkins of this tree serve as a major food source. In the spring (from about March to early June) male birds mark territory by making a distinctive "hoot" noise while perched on a downed long.

Figure 72. Blue Grouse

White and Red-Breasted Nuthatch
        Searching for insects, these birds are rather easily identified by their tendency to forage upside down, walking headfirst down the trunk of a tree. The white-breasted nuthatch is more commonly seen in riparian areas and deciduous forests while the red-breasted nuthatch is more common in coniferous forests, especially among tall fir trees

Figure 73 White- (left) and Red-Breasted (Right) Nuthatches

Figure 74. Pileated Woodpecker

and in thickets of lodge-pole pine. Both typically nest in dead snags or rotten wood, either excavating their own holes or sometimes using holes bored by woodpeckers. The white-breasted nuthatch is the most widely-distributed of those found in North America, likely because of its ecological adaptability.

Pileated Woodpecker

A truly impressive, crow-sized, crested wood-pecker, the pileated wood-pecker is sometimes spotted in the coniferous forests of region, more commonly near water. The bird is predominantly black with some white and a bright red, pointed crest found on both sexes. It often nests in dead snags, and picks sites from 15 to 70 feet above the ground and where the tree is at least 15 inches in diameter. It is a permanent resident, occupying the same territory year after year. This woodpecker feeds mainly on ants and beetle larvae, and its drilling into dead or diseased trees looking for food can be heard seemingly for miles. It seems to prefer feeding on grand fir in the region's mixed-conifer forests.

Three-Toed Woodpecker and Black-Backed Woodpeckers

These very similar woodpeckers, which frequent burned over conifer forests in the region, are distinctive for woodpeckers in having a yellow crown. About three-quarters of the bird's diet consists of bark-boring beetles which attack burnt-over snags following fires. Unlike many woodpeckers, these species commonly tear away the bark of a tree looking for food, rather than drilling holes. The holes the birds do excavate are often used by other avifauna, including bluebirds and nuthatches, when the birds leave an area, which usually occurs four or five years after a fire. The three-toed woodpecker has a black and white barred back, while the other's back is entirely black, distinguishing the species. Due to the quiet nature of the birds and their black coloring, they can be difficult to see in a fire-blackened forest.

Vaux Swift

This dark gray swift, with a cigar-shaped body and slightly paler underside, can be found in woodlands near rivers or lakes in the region. It nests in hollow trees or sometimes along cliffs. The swift's habitat in this region has been degraded, and populations have dwindled. It is now considered a threatened species in the area.

Northern Goshawk

A magnificent bird of prey, the northern goshawk is unfortunately an increasingly rare resident of the dense conifer forests of the Wallowas. The bird's preferred habitat, large areas of old-growth forest, has been heavily damaged, fragmented, or eliminated by intense log-

Figure 75. Northern Goshawk

ging and grazing in most of the region. The northern goshawk is the largest accipter in North America, sometimes feeding on fairly large prey, including grouse and hares. The bird often breeds in old-growth conifer forests near water, but otherwise ranges downward into sagebrush steppe and riparian habitats.

Yellow-Rumped Warbler

The yellow-rumped warbler is very common in the montane forests of the Wallowas from the ponderosa pine forest of middle elevations up to the subalpine forests near timberline. It is mostly bluish-gray above and white below, but has distinctive yellow patches on its rump, crown, throat, and wings.

Western Tanager

This colorful neo-tropical migrant can be seen during the summer throughout the coniferous forests of the Wallowas. The male is the only predominantly yellow bird found in the region, with a reddish head and black wings and tail. The female is duller with yellow below, a greenish-yellow back, and white wing bars. These birds appear to prefer open forested habitat with widely spaced trees rather than dense forests with a thick overstory.

Figure 76. Great-Horned Owl

Great-Horned Owl

The largest of the eared owls, the Great-horned owl can be two feet long with a wingspan of four feet. It is common in the coniferous forests of the area as well as near streams and lakes. It is a powerful and adaptable predator, preying on numerous small mammals and avifauna. It is a major predator of peregrine falcons, and is known to kill coots and ducks as well.

Hermit Thrush

This bird, with its truly beautiful, flute-like song, is a summer resident of mixed-conifer and subalpine forests of the Wallowas. The hermit thrush prefers the shady and moist environment of dense coniferous forest, and is much more commonly heard than seen. Its magnificent song is often heard at dusk. The bird nests on the ground, typically in well-concealed mosses, or on the lower limbs of trees. If seen, the thrush has a densely spotted breast, eye-ring, and a rust-colored tail. A solitary bird, this thrush, like the American robin, feeds on the ground. It is a common summer visitor, migrating to Mexico for the winter.

Other Common Species of Mixed-Conifer Forests

Northern Oriole	Williamson's Sapsucker
Yellow Warbler	Spruce Grouse
Black-Headed Grosbeak	Blue Grouse
Warbling and Solitary Vireo	Chipping Sparrow
White-Crowned Sparrow	Townsend's Warbler

Wildlife of Subalpine Forests

Subalpine forest habitat occurs in the region from 6000 feet to about 7500 feet, where the forest begins to thin into scattered groves amid small meadows and rock outcrops. This forest consists largely of two trees, whitebark pine and subalpine fir, and forests vary from dense, shady stands to open, sunny groves with a rich understory. This habitat is cool and moist throughout the year, and the frost-free growing season at these elevations is usually only about two months. This leaves little time for plants to grow new shoots, distribute seed, and get seedlings underway. Nonetheless, some plants thrive in the environment.

The evergreen conifers of the subalpine forest offer thermal cover in winter for some species, such as the blue grouse, and welcome shade and relief from summer thunderstorms for elk, deer, and bighorn sheep. Red crossbill, pine grosbeak, Clark's nutcrackers, and several species of squirrels and chipmunks feed on whitebark pine seeds in the forest, while hummingbirds can be seen feeding on blossoms in subalpine meadows along the edges of the forest.

Pika

These small brownish black and gray mammals live among the many talus slopes of the Wallowas and other Blue Mountain ranges. One can often hear their high-pitched chirp when hiking through rocky areas. This bleat is a signal to others in the colony of potential danger and commonly results in a few scampering into holes among the rocks. Although pikas live in these colonies they are strongly territorial. Agile and well adapted to their habitat niche, pikas are herbivorous, feeding on forbs, grasses, and shrubs that grow among the rocks.

Figure 77. Pika

They do not hibernate but store in crevices in their rocky habitat supplies of forage gathered in the late summer and fall for winter use.

Red Crossbill

A common year-round bird in the coniferous forests of the region. The males are variably red while the females are mostly yellowish-green. Both have distinctive beaks with crossed tips. Breeding

Figure 78. Red Crossbill

Figure 79. Clark's Nutcracker

usually occurs in pines, mostly lodgepole and ponderosa. The bird migrates to lower elevations in the fall and returns to the higher country as the snows melt in spring.

Clark's Nutcracker

The Clark's Nutcracker is the curious black, gray, and white bird so common in the subalpine forests of the Wallowas. Loud, bold, and busy, the Clark's Nutcracker grows to about a foot in length and feeds predominantly on pine seeds of the whitebark pine. The bird's sharp, heavy bill is an effective tool in prying the seeds from the tree's cones. When the seeds of conifers ripen in the fall, the bird collects hundreds of them, eating some while caching the rest in the ground for future consumption. Studies have shown that the nutcracker can remember up to a thousand seed caches from one season to the next, and that these caches are marked by their relation to landmarks such as rocks or perhaps trees. The birds generally stay in the same area, recovering caches throughout the winter months.

As mentioned earlier, there is an interesting relationship between the Clark's Nutcracker and the whitebark pine, its main source of food.   Studies have shown that about one in three seed caches buried by the bird goes unrecovered, and these seeds often sprout into new trees. The bird's ability to carry many seeds at one time and its tendency to bury them at the perfect depth for germination appears to be an evolutionary co-adaptation with the pine. The pines on the other hand have developed cone structures and fruiting times, which enhance the chance of the seeds being buried by the nutcracker.

Pine Grosbeak

Breeding in the sub-alpine forests of the range during the summer months, the pine grosbeak is a permanent resident of the forests of the Wallowas. It is about the size of an American robin, and has distinctive double-white wing bars on its black wings, with the male having a reddish and the female an olive-colored head, back, and breast.   The female is yellow, and appears to be

Figure 80. Pine Grosbeak

unrelated to the male. The bird usually nests in conifers such as sub-alpine fir and Englemann spruce, especially in open or scattered stands near meadows or streams. It primarily feeds on conifer seeds, insects, buds, and berries.

Great Gray Owl

This rare and elusive owl lives at higher elevations in the Wallowas, feeding on mice, voles, and other rodents. It is a superb predator, crashing on its prey from above through the snow. The great gray owl is one of the largest and most beautiful of the North American owls, though it is rarely seen. It often perches near the trunks of large conifers during the day, remaining motionless and silent. On occasion it may perch at the edge of a clearing, looking for prey. It has a large, grayish body and an "earless" head with a distinctive white "mustache" marking. It is considered threatened in the region.

Other Common Species of Subalpine Forests

Columbian Ground Squirrel	Elk
Snowshoe Hare	Spruce Grouse
Northern Goshawk	Black Bear

Wildlife of Open Subalpine and Alpine Tundra

This habitat occurs from about 8000 feet to nearly 10,000 feet, depending on local factors such as soil type and slope aspect. Open subalpine terrain can include scattered trees, lush meadows, and rocky slopes near the tundra/forest ecotone, while true alpine tundra habitat occurs only on the highest peaks above 9000 feet.

Mountain Goat

Sometimes, when hiking among the rugged peaks of the High Wallowas, one may hear the crash of rocks tumbling down a cliff face to the valley below. Closer inspection may reveal the source of the noise; a group of white hairy objects perched on some extraordinarily steep mountainside seemingly oblivious to any danger. These are the Wallowas' mountain goats, sauntering along the crests of the ranges' high peaks. Introduced to the area in 1950, some debate exists as to whether they are native to the region.

Mountain goats live in an environment where few other large animals can survive. Their heavy white coats, which protect them from cold winds and snow so common in their high elevation habitat, coupled with their wide range of food selection enables them to live year round in subalpine and alpine areas where most other animals could not survive. Though the goats' wool coats do offer excellent insulation, they are less effective when wet. Therefore goats often utilize overhanging cliffs or shallow caves for shelter. Here the animals can stay relatively dry during prolonged stormy periods.

The goats have few serious predators. Their superb mountaineering ability allows them to evade many potential predators by simply walking up along steep ridges and above massive cliffs where other animals wouldn't dare go. There sharp, dagger-like horns can also serve as a deterrent.

Mountain goats feed primarily on grasses and forbs, but sometimes browse on shrubs as well, especially in the winter when other food sources are scarce.

The mountain goats in the Wallowas prefer the steep rocky slopes of Chief Joseph Mountain and the Hurricane Divide, and sometimes one can see small herds grazing on the short grasses of these and other subalpine and alpine areas. In addition to the Wallowas, mountain goats have also been transplanted into the Elkhorn Mountains across the Powder River valley to the west.

Rocky Mountain Bighorn Sheep

The large area of rugged country encompassing the High Wallowas and the nearby Hells Canyon of the Snake River supports a number of Rocky Mountain Bighorn Sheep herds. The precipitous bunchgrass covered slopes so common in the area offer ideal habitat for these graceful sheep. Some of these ranges are also grazed by domestic sheep, and there have been problems with bighorns contracting fatal diseases spread by these non-native inhabitants.

Bighorn sheep disappeared from the Wallowa-Hells Canyon area by the middle 1940s as a result of both disease and overharvest. In 1971 a heard of 20, transplanted from Jasper National Park in the Canadian Rockies, were reintroduced into the Hells Canyon area but disappeared just two years later. A second herd, released the same year in the Lostine River valley in the Wallowa high country, was more successful and is the basis for the current herd in the region.

In the summer, migratory sheep can sometimes be spotted in subalpine meadows and among the alpine peaks of the High

Figure 81. Rocky Mountain Bighorn Sheep

Wallowas. The lush grasses of the mountains offer excellent summer range for the herds. Bighorn sheep are amazingly agile, and must be to negotiate the rough terrain of the higher peaks. The sheep run across large boulder fields as if they were grassy lawns and teeter calmly on sides of cliffs to nibble succulent grasses oblivious to any danger. Only the mountain goat rivals the sheep in mountaineering prowess.

The United States Forest Service is currently involved in an extensive bighorn sheep disease research, population monitoring, and transplant program in the Wallowa/Hells Canyon region. The Foundation for North American Wild Sheep has committed 10 million dollars over the next 10 years to help fund the project.

Wallowa Rosy Finch

This small, alpine finch, a local race of rosy finch, can sometimes be seen at higher elevations in the range though it is not an abundant species. The bird has a gray crown and its rump, underparts, and wings have a rosy tint. During the breeding season it inhabits alpine areas in the high cirques of the range, nesting among talus slopes and cliffs and foraging on frozen insects. During the fall and winter it moves to lower elevations surrounding the range, including sagebrush steppe, grasslands, and pasturelands.

Calliope Hummingbird

A truly tiny bird, the calliope hummingbird has a wingspan of just 3 inches. It prefers open areas adjacent to coniferous forests, frequenting areas vegetated with willow or sagebrush. Later in the summer it can be spotted in subalpine and alpine meadows of many Blue Mountain ranges.

The male bird has a distinctive striped gorget of iridescent scarlet and white, while the females are best recognized by their tiny size and cinnamon underparts.

Wildlife of Riparian Areas

Riparian areas can be found at nearly all elevations in the area, from the Snake River at 800 feet above sea level in Hells Canyon to cool mountain streams originating in the high basins of the Wallowas. These areas, with their diversity of both coniferous and broadleaf trees and available water, are important to most of the region's wildlife.

Whitetail Deer

Whitetail Deer are common in the agricultural lands and streamside habitats of the Wallowa Valley on the north side of the mountains. Unlike mule deer populations in the region, the whitetail population appears to be on the increase. They prefer lower elevation habitat than the mule deer and are not seen in the higher basins of the High Wallowas.

Beaver

Though nearly trapped to extinction throughout the mountain West in the 1800s, the beaver is still a resident of some riparian areas in the Blues. In the Wallowas they are most common along the Lostine River on the north end of the range.

Figure 82. Beaver

Beavers use their strong teeth to chop down streamside trees such as willow, aspen, and cottonwood, to construct small woody dams, forming ponds. These flooded areas allow access to food supplies without too much exposure to potential predators. Dams are commonly plastered tight with mud, and in some areas may be constructed of gravel and stones in addition to downed wood. Beavers living along larger, free-flowing rivers or streams live in burrows on the banks rather than in dams.

The beaver feeds primarily on leaves and cambium of trees or on aquatic vegetation. They store their food underwater embedding branches into the bottom of their constructed ponds.

Beavers are active in the late afternoon and throughout the night and remain so throughout the year. Where rivers and ponds freeze over the beaver depends on food collected and stored underneath the ice.

Spotted Sandpiper
The small spotted sandpiper is often seen along watercourses, most commonly at lower elevations. It is fairly easily recognized by its distinctive up and down bobbing motion, although another common bird of aquatic environments, the dipper or water ouzel, also engages in this nervous-looking twitch. The bird prefers shaded riparian areas. Interestingly, female sandpipers are the first migrants during spring to

breeding grounds. Here they establish nesting territory and compete for harems of males who arrive later.

Dipper

A small, gray, wren-like bird, the dipper is commonly seen bobbing about in the mountain streams of the region. It cocks its tail like a wren, and is often spotted flying quickly just above the water's surface or tip-toeing on and about shoreline rocks. It forages underwater, eating insects dislodged from the cobbles of the streambed. The dipper is highly territorial, sometimes building nests on rocks behind waterfalls but more often on wood bridges which cross creeks or rivers.

Common Merganser

Males of this species are mostly white but with a greenish-black crested head and a bright red bill. Females are smaller and mostly brown in color. The bird preys on fish, and is commonly seen along rivers and near lakes and reservoirs. One of the most beautiful and

Figure 83. Common Merganser

elegant of North American waterfowl, this, the largest of the mergansers, is a year-round resident in the region.

Belted Kingfisher

The belted kingfisher has a distinctive bluish crested head and white underparts. It is always found near water, hovering and periodically plunging into streams or lakes to feed on small fish. It nests in exposed earthen surfaces such as eroded banks and sometimes roadcuts near riparian areas.

The bird hunts by sight, capturing fish with its long, pointed beak after hovering for sometime searching out its prey. Mature kingfishers teach their young how to fish by first capturing their prey, beating the poor fish until it is nearly dead, and then throwing it back into the water so the younger bird can capture the fish by itself.

Figure 84. Belted Kingfisher

Other Species Common to Riparian Areas

Veery/Gray catbird
Bank Swallow
Tree Sparrow
Yellow Warbler
Warbling Vireo
Red-Eyed Vireo
Goldeneye
Wood Duck
Teal

Canada Goose
Upland Sandpiper
Whistling Swan
Bald Eagle
Swainson's Thrush
Rainbow Trout
Dolly Varden Trout
Brook Trout
Salmon

EAGLE CAP WILDERNESS TRAILS

Wilderness Use

Maintained by the United States Forest Service, the extensive trail system of the Wallowas includes over 500 miles of backcountry trails, most of which are partly or wholly within the Eagle Cap Wilderness area. Most visitors enter the wilderness from three popular trailheads along the northern side of the range. Access is slightly more difficult in the western, southern, and eastern parts of the range. These areas are subsequently less traveled, offering hikers and horseback riders more solitude than the central and northern Wallowas.

A survey study undertaken by Hall and Shelby (1994) of Oregon State University on use of the Eagle Cap Wilderness Area has revealed some interesting information on wilderness visitation. Almost 75% of wilderness visitors travel on foot with the rest on livestock, and 70% of all visitors take only day trips into the area. 60% of all visitors enter the wilderness at one of three trailheads on the north side of the mountains: Wallowa Lake, Two Pan, or Hurricane Creek. Only 18% of hikers in the wilderness are from northeastern Oregon, while almost 30% come from the Portland-Salem-Eugene area in the Willamette Valley. Use appears to have doubled since the early 1980s, but during this time there has also been a dramatic shift to day use. The number of overnight visitors has actually declined somewhat during this same period. According to the survey, the busiest parts of the wilderness include the Lakes Basin, West Fork Wallowa River, the East Fork Lostine River, Hurricane Creek, and the Copper Creek/Swamp Lake area. Of the visitors surveyed in the summer and fall of 1993, 34% were on their first trip into the Eagle Cap Wilderness, further indication of the area's increasing popularity.

Region by Region Guide

The following is a brief guide to some of the natural features found in different areas of the Wallowa Mountains. The range can be divided into the following physiographic regions: the lower Minam River/Bear Creek area, the upper Minam River valley, the Elkhorn Peak/Steamboat Lake region, the Lostine River/Hurricane Creek area, the Wallowa River region, the Big Sheep region, the Lakes Basin, the northern Imnaha Basin, the southern Imnaha Basin, and the Eagle Creek area. For further information on the trails of the Wallowas see *Hiking the High Wallowas and Hells Canyon*, edited by Frank Conley and published by Pika Press and *Hiking Oregon's Eagle Cap Wilderness* by Fred Barstad.

The lower Minam River/Bear Creek area

This region includes the deep canyons and rolling forested ridges of the extreme western and northwestern Wallowas along the drainages of Bear Creek, Trout Creek, Murphy Creek, and the lower Minam River. This area is notable for its rare, low elevation wilderness scenery along the rivers and creeks draining this portion of the range.

The Minam River valley is wholly within the Eagle Cap Wilderness for approximately 35 miles, from its source at Blue Lake west of Eagle Cap to the wilderness boundary southeast of State Highway 82. There are a few parcels of private land along this stretch, though Red's Horse Ranch, about 10 miles into the wilderness from the northwest, was recently purchased by the Forest Service. The upper half of the valley has been glacially scoured and is characteristically U-shaped, while the lower half has been carved into a steep-sided V-shaped canyon by the rushing waters of this beautiful river. The canyons of the other principal streams in the area also have steep sides from 1000 to 2000 feet high. Though the valley bottoms are heavily forested with a mix of ponderosa pine, Douglas-fir, western larch, and grand fir, south facing exposures along the canyon walls are mostly open grasslands. The narrow ridgetops are generally lightly forested or open parklands, whitebark pine and subalpine fir the dominant species above 7,000 feet.

Most of the rocks in this area are basalt of the Columbia River Basalt Group. These basalts uncomformably overlie the Wallowa Batholith, indicating that uplift and subsequent erosion of the range had revealed the granitic core before eruption of these basalts. These lavas likely covered the entire range at one point, but now are mostly found along the western ridges and canyons, as scattered remnants on some higher peaks, and as the principal bedrock of the Wallowa and Grande Ronde valleys to the north and west. The horizontally layered basalts comprise the lower areas of this region of the wilderness, and are well exposed along the steep valley walls of the many canyons. Further to the east and higher in elevation the granodiorite of the Wallowa Batholith can be seen in some areas along the valley floors and the higher ridges. Along the crest of Jim White Ridge an outcrop of an enigmatic gravel unit (see p. 45) covers almost a square mile. This gravel includes rounded boulders, some larger than 2 feet in diameter, and clasts which may have been derived from metamorphic rocks to the east in west-central Idaho and deposited here *before* the formation of Hells Canyon.

The upper Minam River Valley

This area includes the small lakes and high ridges along north side of the Upper Minam Basin.

Forming the west side of the upper Minam valley is a long somewhat arcuate ridgeline running east-west and extending from China Cap on the west past several peaks to Needle Point and on to

Frazier Pass at its eastern end. The ridge remains above 8000 feet for most of its approximately 12 mile length, and several subalpine and alpine lakes lie below the crest on its northern and southern sides. A few trails lead over passes to these lakes and along the divide, offering close-up views of the craggy peaks as well as sweeping vistas of the heavily forested Minam River valley far below and the rest of the High Wallowas to the north and east. Along this divide are some impressive rock walls, especially along the north side of Needle Point. These are several hundred feet high and are carved out of sound granitic rock of the Wallowa Batholith.

This area is predominantly granodiorite of the Wallowa Batholith. China Cap and Burger Butte, at the southwestern margin of the area, are composed of Columbia River basalt, and are noticeably brown compared to the whitish gray of the peaks to the east. Distinctive Brown Mountain rises above the waters of Blue Lake at the headwaters of the Minam River west of Eagle Cap, a remnant of the Columbia River Basalt Group. Below China Cap's steep north face are a series of moraines which, because of their subdued weathered appearance and vegetative cover, have been classified as Glacier Lake deposits dating to approximately 10,000 years ago.

Some of the most rugged terrain in the Wallowas can be found along the ridge running from Needle Point to China Cap. Cliffs hundreds of feet high, extensive talus slopes, shady, lush subalpine forests, and great relief characterize this not-often visited region. Pleistocene glaciers have carved large, deep cirque basins, some over 2500 feet deep, below Needle Point and other high points in the area. More recent glaciation of the Holocene has left conspicuous Neoglacial moraines in some areas. A well-developed and fairly long moraine extends towards Little Pop Lake from the crest of Needle Point.

The Elkhorn Peak/Steamboat Lake region

This region encompasses an area of lakes and peaks above North Minam Meadows and on the divide west of the West Fork of the Lostine River.

Figure 85. The lush headwaters of Copper Creek.

Elkhorn Peak and Glacier Mountain are the highest peaks in this area, both rising above 9,000 feet, while Flagstaff Point, Minam Peak, and several others rise above 8,000 feet. Most of the lakes of the area are in basins forested with stands of lodgepole and whitebark pine.

The area is almost all granodiorite of the Wallowa Batholith, but a few scattered outcrops of the Columbia River Basalt Group and the Tertiary Gravel exist near a small, high plateau north of Granite Gulch.

North Minam Meadows lies in a beautiful valley of the North Fork Minam River a few miles below the high cirque containing Steamboat Lake. This large, lush meadow has some excellent campsites and is generally not too crowded. The meadow offers panoramic views of the peaks enclosing the river valley.

The Lostine River/Hurricane Creek area
This area includes the trails along the two forks of the Lostine River, the Hurricane Divide, the Hurricane Creek trail, and the Sacajawea Peak region.

Figure 86. Looking northward down the East Fork Lostine River valley.

The upper valley of the East Fork Lostine River is one of the more pleasant areas of the range, the river meandering through a very large meadow with a nice view of the dome of Eagle Cap at the head of the valley. This meadow near the headwaters of the Lostine is the largest in the range.

The massive ridge rising to the east above the Lostine River Road is the Hurricane Divide, a row of sharp peaks separating the East Fork of the Lostine River from Hurricane Creek. A trail to Frances Lake leaves the Lostine River Road several miles before the road's end at the Two Pan campground and trailhead. This trail climbs over 3000 feet to the Frances Lake basin, a large alpine valley below the 9,000 foot ridges and peaks of the Hurricane Divide. This basin is one of the more alpine in the range, with much of the area around and above Frances Lake tundra or bare rock. Along this trail one passes through many of the principal rocks comprising the Wallowas; the Hurwal Fm., the Martin Bridge Fm., the Clover Creek Greenstone, and the Wallowa Batholith. Most of the northern Hurricane Divide is composed of the Hurwal, Martin Bridge, and Clover Creek rocks, while the southern divide is all granitic rocks of the Wallowa Batholith. A craggy peak rising to 9386 feet near the southern end of the Hurricane Divide, has a few small permanent snowfields and several Neoglacial moraines below its northeastern face. Just to the south and east of Frances Lake, the divide is composed of marble of the Martin Bridge Formation. This area around Deadman Lake is nearly devoid of trees, as most conifers struggle to establish themselves in the poorly developed soil characteristic of much of the Martin Bridge Formation.

The Hurricane Creek valley is fairly open, especially at its lower and upper ends, offering views of the highest peaks in the range. Avalanche chutes are common along the steep walls of the valley. The creek was apparently named Hurricane because the sound of rolling boulders in the creek during spring run-off reminded some early settlers, may of whom were from the Southeast, of the sounds of a hurricane. The flattened areas of trees found along the length of the creek, a result of massive avalanches, look as if a hurricane may have roared through the canyon causing the damage. Some of the more prominent peaks along the valley walls include Chief Joseph Mountain, Sacajawea, and the Matterhorn on the east side of the valley and Twin Peaks along the Hurricane Divide to the west.

The rocks of the lower Hurricane Creek valley are predominantly those of the Martin Bridge Formation and the Hurwal Formation of the Upper Triassic and Lower Jurassic Lucile Group. Excellent exposures of the Martin Bridge can be seen along both sides of the Hurricane Creek valley. The very steep walls of the Deadman Creek area on the west side of the lower valley are Martin Bridge, and the north and west faces of Sacajawea and the Matterhorn farther up the valley are composed primarily of this formation. The limestone has been metamorphosed and has recrystallized into a coarse, light gray marble. Two periods of metamorphism have dramatically changed the structure and appearance of the Martin Bridge Formation found in this area of the range as compared to the type locality farther to the south along Eagle Creek.

The Wallowa River region

This region includes the West and East Forks of the Wallowa River, the Matterhorn/Ice Lake area, and to the east the Bonny Lakes/McCully Basin area.

Ice Lake lies in a large glacial depression surrounded by numerous peaks and smaller cirques, the Matterhorn situated directly to the west, almost 2000 feet above lake level. The Matterhorn is a relatively easy climb from the lake, as broad ridges between the sheer faces of the peak are class 2 climbs. The mountain is composed of highly deformed Martin Bridge Limestone, the southeast and northeast sides of the peak bright gray marble walls hundreds of feet high. Shaded by the 500 foot-high northeast face of the peak, a steep snowfield remains throughout the year, complete with Neoglacial moraines along its northern side (lateral) and at its base (terminal). A small rock glacier lies just below these moraines. This above timberline basin situated below the alpine face of the Matterhorn and the massive Hurwal Divide is easily one of the more dramatic of those found in the range. The cirque along the southeast side of the Matterhorn lies below a broad bright wall hundreds of feet high of Martin Bridge marble. The marble is highly contorted and several dark shale layers are visible forming sinuous snake-like patterns across the face of the peak. A talus slope consisting almost entirely of coarse weathered calcite grains drapes the lower part of the headwall to the cirque floor.

Above the southern shore of the lake the granitic slopes of Craig Mountain rise to 9,000 feet. The eastern shore of the lake is bounded by a relatively smooth, glacially scoured bedrock outcrop of granodiorite. Near the lake's outlet a Columbia River Basalt dike cuts across the granodiorite. The small tree-covered promontory jutting out into Ice Lake is closed to camping for rehabilitation of the natural vegetation.

The trail up the West Fork Wallowa River canyon travels mostly through heavily forested terrain, offering only glimpses here and there of the massive walls bounding the narrow valley. The more open section of the West Fork trail near Frazier Lake is exceptionally scenic,

however. Absolutely huge cliffs of Martin Bridge limestone rise directly above the floor of the valley to the south and east, and the sparsely
forested marshy area around Frazier Lake affords nice views of the
upper basin. At certain times of the year a waterfall cascades down the
sides of the surrounding cliffs. Frazier Lake often has large "snowbergs" floating in its waters, as avalanches deposit exceptionally large
amounts of snow in the lake which linger beyond the break up of the
winter ice cover.

The trail branching off to the west towards the Lakes Basin has
several fine viewpoints of the upper West Fork Wallowa River valley.
The limestone walls of Sentinel Peak and the horn of Cusick
Mountain at the head of the valley rise steeply more than 2500 feet
above the lush subalpine meadows and Frazier Lake.

Situated at the head of the West Fork Wallowa River valley,
Glacier Lake and its alpine cirque may be the most scenic area in the
entire range. The southeast ridge of Eagle Cap and the point of
Glacier Peak rise 1300 feet above the deep blue waters of the lake.
Scattered whitebark pines grow on the eastern shore of the lake and
on several small, picturesque islands, while a large, blocky rock wall
bounds the southern shoreline. The barren slopes of the high peaks,
the shimmering ice and snow of the Benson snowfield, formerly the
range's only active glacier, and the large moraines found in the area
give the lake and its surroundings an alpine feel. The steep-sided
mounds of boulders just above the southwest shore of the lake are
terminal moraines of the Eagle Cap Neoglacial advance. Some of
these moraines are less than 100 years old, indicating that very
recently the Benson snowfield extended much farther down the
cirque and was actively depositing glacial debris just above the shores
of the lake.

The East Fork Wallowa River valley is one of the shorter principal drainages of the range, extending roughly 8 miles from the river's
headwaters near Aneroid Mountain to the West Fork junction just
above Wallowa Lake. The trail from the Wallowa trailhead to Aneroid
Lake is one of the more popular day hikes in the range, climbing nearly 3000 feet in about 6 miles.

Above the East Fork valley and in areas to the east Columbia River Basalt remains along the higher ridges, unlike most of the High Wallowas where this rock has been eroded away. The flat-lying, horizontally layered lavas can be seen all along the valley's eastern wall, deposited on granitic rocks of the Wallowa Batholith. The dome of 9,700 foot Aneroid Mountain is composed of Columbia River Basalt and is easily recognized at the head of the valley. The trail travels across granitic bedrock to Aneroid Lake before passing rocks of the Hurwal and Martin Bridge Formations near Tenderfoot Pass.

The East Fork Wallowa River valley is quite heavily forested for much of its length. At the foot of talus slopes and in small openings in the lower valley broadleaf trees are common and include quaking aspen, black cottonwood, vine maple, and dogwood. Grand fir and Douglas-fir are the principal conifers. Higher up subalpine fir dominates the valley floor, with lodgepole pine abundant at several marshy areas and around Aneroid Lake. The forest cover thins quickly above Aneroid Lake, and whitebark pine becomes more abundant to timberline.

The Big Sheep region

The Bonny Lakes area and much of the Big Sheep Creek drainage are quite distinct from most of the rest of the range. Here Columbia River Basalt comprises many of the higher peaks, including Aneroid Mountain. Outcrops of the Hurwal Formation can be seen along the southern rim of the Bonny Lakes valley. The Bonny Lakes lie in a gentle subalpine basin and are surrounded by open meadows and wildflower fields. Mountain willows cover many of the wetter, marshy areas. At slightly lower elevations (7,000 feet) extensive stands of Lodgepole Pine carpet the valley floor. The trail up the Big Sheep Creek drainage begins in a recently burned area. The high-intensity Canal Fire of 1988 burned thousands of acres along the northeastern edge of the range. Today this area is carpeted with young lodgepole pine saplings.

The Lakes Basin

Mirror Lake, at the western edge of the Lakes Basin, is one of the most popular lakes in the wilderness. The view of the north side of Eagle Cap over the reflective waters of the lake is spectacular. Several small tarns are situated just above the steep cliffs on the south side of the lake, directly below the granodiorite dome of Eagle Cap. Eagle Cap has a few small permanent snowfields on its northern flank in addition to several Neoglacial moraines and a rock glacier.

Mirror Lake and the other lakes in the basin, among them Moccassin, Horseshoe, and Crescent, are all underlain by granodiorite of the Wallowa Batholith. Dark basalt dikes can be seen in a few areas cutting through the granitic rock, as on the north face of Eagle Cap. This area was heavily glaciated during the Wisconsin Period, and was the sight of a large neve field that fed glaciers of the East Fork Lostine, Hurricane, and West Fork Wallowa valleys.

The northern Imnaha Basin

This area includes the isolated valleys of the Middle and North Forks of the Imnaha River east of Cusick Mountain and Sentinel Peak and the Tenderfoot Pass/Bonny Lakes area. The eastern Wallowas differ markedly from the central and western parts of the range. The region is underlain mostly by darker sedimentary, volcanic, and metamorphic rocks rather than the bright Wallowa Batholith, the topography is more subdued, and there are few lakes, though there are many rivers and streams. This area, particularly the upper reaches of the Middle Fork of the Imnaha River, is seldom visited.

North Fork Imnaha River valley/Tenderfoot Pass

The North Fork Imnaha River valley is one of the less frequented principal valleys of the range. Looking across the valley from the trail running west from the Imnaha Divide, one notices the cliff-forming Martin Bridge Formation along the lower half of the prominent ridge immediately to the south. This resistant, grayish white limestone forms a distinctly different topography than the overlying Hurwal Formation. The Hurwal Formation forms a more subdued, rolling topography with extensive scree slopes rather than bedrock faces and cliffs. Most of the higher peaks in this region are comprised of the Hurwal Formation (except Pete's Point) and they are noticeably smoother and less rugged than other parts of the range. Several narrow avalanche chutes extend to the valley floor from the steep north-facing ridges, periodically clearing small meadows along the length of the river. These frequent avalanches are constantly pruning the small subalpine firs growing in their paths to a height of about 4 feet. A sparse woodland of whitebark pine at higher elevations and Douglas-fir at lower elevations grows along the ridge which bounds the north side of the valley.

The southern Imnaha Basin

This area includes the South Fork Imnaha River valley to Hawkins Pass, the Cliff Creek drainage, and the Pine Lakes/Red Mountain area.

Krag Peak, just west of Crater Lake, supports an active rock glacier in a small cirque below the peak's northeast face. This rock glacier has a characteristically steep front of boulders.

South Fork Imnaha River Valley/ Hawkins Pass

Unlike many of the valleys in the High Wallowas, the South Fork Imnaha River valley trends east-west and is carved almost entirely out of rocks of the Clover Creek Greenstone, the Martin Bridge Formation, and the Hurwal Formation. The bedrock type and orientation have led to slightly different topography and vegetation patterns in this area. Heading in a spectacular cirque basin surrounded by the sheer marble walls of Cusick Mountain, the South Fork Imnaha River flows west for a short bit before swinging to the south and then flowing east for most of its length out of the range. Unlike some of the narrower, steeper drainages, this valley is fairly broad with a gently sloping valley floor.

The Eagle Creek area

This region includes the main Eagle Creek, East Eagle Creek

and West Eagle Creek and the spectacular lakes and ridges above these drainages.

The valleys of West Eagle Creek and the main Eagle Creek are cut into Wallowa Batholith granodiorite. The divide between the West Fork and East Fork of Eagle Creek is capped by the rusty brown shales and sandstones of the Hurwal Formation. The rocks along the east slope of this divide, across the East Fork valley, and up onto the ridge of Krag Peak have been so severely folded they have been over-turned. The Martin Bridge lies conformably above the Hurwal, indi-cating that tectonic forces have flipped the rocks over, this perhaps occurring during the collision and accretion process of the Wallowa Terrane. Overlying these two formations of the Lucile Group is the Clover Creek Greenstone.

West Eagle Creek

From West Eagle Meadows a moderate trail leads to Echo and Traverse Lakes, a group of beautiful **paternoster lakes**. These fairly large lakes are situated in a lush hanging valley and are surrounded by steep granitic cliffs, fields of wildflowers, and open subalpine forests of subalpine fir and whitebark pine with some Englemann spruce in wet-ter areas along the floor of the valley.

Main Eagle Creek

The main Eagle Creek valley is one of the more popular drainages of the southern Wallowas, though it is still not as visited as the principal valleys of the northern range. The main fork of Eagle Creek, heading in Eagle Lake, flows through several meadows and a steep gorge on its way out of the mountains. Western larch can be seen mingling with subalpine fir and Englemann spruce at elevations above 6500 feet, and some very large trees stand far above the surrounding conifers.

East Fork of Eagle Creek

The East Fork Eagle Creek valley is easily one of the most spec-tacular in the range. This narrow U-shaped trough is a textbook glacial valley. Throughout most of its length the walls of the canyon rise steeply thousands of feet above the valley floor. The southern entrance to the canyon near the East Eagle trailhead is bounded by huge limestone cliffs on the west and the precipitous slopes of 9000 foot Krag Peak on the east, and from here to Frazier and Horton passes the East Eagle trail travels through beautiful, mostly open terrain. Large avalanche chutes stream down the sides of the valley into large open grassy areas and a few flat park-like meadows. These chutes are often strewn with broken limbs and very large trunks, evidence of the power of moving snow. The lower trail follows the east side of the creek, passing in and out of stands of grand fir with occasional occurrences of ponderosa pine, Douglas-fir, and western larch. Some of the groves of grand fir contain many large trees 3 feet in diameter near their trunks and a few over 4 feet in diameter. Douglas-fir is more common on the sunnier west-facing side of the valley, while Western larch can be found intermittently to about 5200 feet. The trail climbs gradually above the roaring stream, passing a few waterfalls and a number of tributary streams. The upper portion of the valley above 6000 feet is moderately forested with subalpine fir, whose narrow spire-like crowns reach heights of nearly 100 feet. Some fairly large stands of this hearty fir occur on northeast facing slopes below Hidden and Moon Lakes and near Frazier Pass. A group of large cottonwoods near the Hidden Lake trail junction can be seen growing in a lush opening on the east side of the creek at an elevation of 6000 feet, approaching their upper limit. On the west side of the valley near this junction an avalanche, originating somewhere on the opposite side of the valley, traveled upslope a few hundred feet, knocking down a large area of fir trees. A few areas along the course of the creek are quite flat, and here the creek takes on a braided form flowing through lush grasses and below large cottonwoods. These flat areas develop between narrow gorges as the gradient of the glacially carved valley decreases and the stream slows, depositing some of its sediment load. Eventually sediment from the stream fills these depressions, and a flat area of slower moving water will develop until the stream approaches a steeper gradient, where it will again cut

Figure 87. Looking southward down the glaciated trough of the East Eagle Creek Valley.

down into bedrock. The massive avalanches sweeping down the sides of the valley have prevented conifers from inhabiting much of the valley floor and walls. Waterfalls cascading over small cliffs are common in narrow, steep tributary canyons and are especially beautiful in June and July when these streams are well fed by snowfields on the upper canyon walls.

The rocks along the valley walls below Coon Creek are mostly metamorphosed sedimentary sequences of the Martin Bridge Formation and the Hurwal Formation. Krag Peak is comprised of Clover Creek Greenstone, while the ridge running north from Krag Peak all the way to Jackson Peak is capped with Martin Bridge Formation marble. One can see planar bedding in the rock on some faces above the high cirques along this ridge. Much of the ridge on the west side of the valley is red and brown shales and sandstones of the Hurwal Formation. Above Coon Creek more and more of the Wallowa Batholith is exposed and along the trail one can see the mineralogical variations in the batholith rocks. Some are noticeably dark gray, having a greater percentage of mafic minerals than their more felsic associates. The upper valley is all Wallowa Batholith except the conspicuous basalt dikes of the Columbia River Basalt Group. The horn of Jackson Peak, and much of the ridge to the south, is capped by a prominent cliff of marble. Just north of Jackson Peak is the contact zone of the batholith and the rocks of the Lucile Group. The Eagle Cap-Glacier Peak ridge is composed of granodiorite of the Wallowa Batholith.

Near Dodge Creek a number of dome like outcrops of granitic rock rise above the valley floor. Those higher on the west side show evidence of exfoliation, while much of the rock along and just above Eagle Creek is noticeably smooth and has a sculpted look to it. Here are nice outcrops of glacially polished rock. The older polished rock has a reddish tint due to some oxidation weathering and patches of it stand out from the recently exposed lighter rock of the batholith. Running one's hand across the two different surfaces shows a marked difference in the texture of the rock. The polished rock is exceptionally smooth, while the younger exposures are rougher and bumpier. The grit in the ice of the Eagle glacier acted as sandpaper, abrading and scouring the underlying bedrock into a smooth, polished surface. This glacial polish can be seen on the granitic outcrops along Eagle Creek just below its junction with Dodge Creek.

An additional thanks to:

Stephen Arno, Nancy Langston, Alvin Josephy, William Sullivan, Charles Johnson, Ellen Morris Bishop, Charles Bukowski, Steve Terrill, Jeff Gnass, Ansel Adams, Jerry Franklin, Fred Beckey, J. Krishnamurti, John Muir, Stephen Whitney, Ray Atkeson, William Ashworth, Edward Abbey, Tracy Vallier, Howard Brooks, Bono, Edge, Larry, and Adam, Bobby, Jerry, Phil, Mickey, Bill, Donna, Keith, Brent and Pigpen, Kevin Pogue, Pat O'Hara, Trey, Page, Mike, and Jon, Ric Bailey, Tim Lellebo, Fred Barstad, Peter, Michael, Bill, and Mike, Anne Minard, Todd Wojtowicz, Amy Hatfield, Mark Daniels, Matthew Loeser, James Battin, Desiree Robertson, John and Ingrid, Robert and Bridgette, Barbara Buse, Andy and SuZan Pearce, Steve Monroe, Chris Franznick, the Freaks from the Peaks, Mesa and Jaco, and The Mootsiko.

About the author

KEITH POHS is a native Oregonian whose interest in the natural world began at an early age. While attending Whitman College in Walla Walla, Washington, where he received a Bachelor of Arts in Geology, Keith began to explore northeastern Oregon's beautiful Wallowa Mountains. Over the last 10 years he has hiked and photographed much of the High Wallowas and the surrounding country. He recently completed a Master of Science in Earth Science at Northern Arizona University in Flagstaff.

APPENDIX

Wildlife species recorded on the Wallowa-Whitman National Forest as compiled by the United States Forest Service.

FISHES

Pacific Lamprey
Western Brook Lamprey
Western Brook Lamprey
White Sturgeon
Chiselmouth
Carp
Peamouth
Northern Squawfish
Bridgelip Sucker
Bluegill
Smallmouth Bass
Largemouth Bass
White Crappie
Yellow Perch
Prickly Sculpin
Chinook Salmon-Summer
Mountain Whitefish
Longnose Dace
Leopard Dace
Malheur Mottled Sculpin
Paiute Sculpin
Torrent Sculpin
Reside Shiner
Brown Bullhead
Channel Catfish
Tadpole Madtom

Golden Trout
Snake River Fine
   -Spotted Cuthroat Trout
Steelhead (Rainbow) Trout
Rainbow Trout
Redband Trout
   Sockeye Salmon
Kokanee
Chinook Salmon-Spring
Chinook Salmon-Fall
Speckled Dace
Brook Trout
Lake Trout
Coho Salmon

AMPHIBIANS

Coeur d'Alene Salamander
Tiger Salamander
Long-Toed Salamander
Woodhouse Toad
Great-Basin
   Spade-Foot Toad
Western Toad
Tailed Frog
Pacific Tree Frog
Spotted Frog
Leopard Frog

REPTILES

Western Fence Lizard
Sagebrush Lizard
Side-Blotched Lizard
Desert Horned Lizard
Western Skink
Western Whiptail
Northern Alligator Lizard
Rubber Boa
Ringneck Snake
Yellow-Bellied Racer
Striped Whipsnake
Gopher Snake
Common Garter Snake
Western Terrestrial
    Garter Snake
Western Ground Snake
Night Snake
Western Pacific Rattlesnake

BIRDS

Arctic Loon
Pied-Billed Grebe
Horned Grebe
Red-Necked Grebe
Eared Grebe
Western Grebe
American White Pelican
Double-Crested Cormorant
American Bittern
Great Blue Heron
Great Egret
Snowy Egret

Cattle Egret
Black-Crowned
    Night Heron
White-Faced Ibis
Tundra Swan
Trumpeter Swan
Mute Swan
Canada Goose
Snow Goose
Ross' Goose
Mallard
Gadwall
American Coot
Western Snowy Plover
Killdeer
Mountain Plover
Common Snipe
Long-billed Curlew
Upland Sandpiper
Spotted Sandpiper
Solitary Sandpiper
Greater Yellowlegs
Lesser Yellowlegs
Willet
Pectoral Sandpiper
Baird's Sandpiper
Least Piper
Western Sandpiper
Long-Billed Dowitcher
American Avocet
Wilson's Phalarope
Herring Gull
California Gull
Ring-Billed Gull
Franklin's Gull
Bonaparte's Gull

Sabine's Gull
Forester's Tern
Caspian Tern
Black Tern
Band-Tailed Pigeon
Rock Dove
Mourning dove
Western Yellow-billed Cuckoo
Common Barn Owl
Western Screech Owl
Flammulated Owl
Great Horned Owl
Snowy Owl
Northern Pygmy Owl
Burrowing Owl
Barred Owl
Great Gray Owl
Long-Eared Owl
Short-Eared Owl
Boreal Owl
Northern Saw-Whet Owl
Common Poorwill
Common Night Hawk
Black Swift
Vaux's Swift
White –Throated Swift
Black-Chinned Hummingbird
Pintail
Green-Winged Teal
Blue-Winged Teal
Cinnamon Teal
European Wigeon
American Wigeon
Northern Shoveler
Wood Duck
Redhead

Ring-Necked Duck
Canvasback
Greater Scaup
Lesser Scaup
Common Golden Eye
Barrow's Golden Eye
Bufflehead
Harlequin Duck
White-winged Scooter
Ruddy duck
Hooded Merganser
Common Merganser
Red-Breasted Merganser
Turkey Vulture
Black-shouldered Kite
Northern Goshawk
Sharp-Shinned Hawk
Coopers Hawk
Red-Tailed Hawk
Rough-Legged Hawk
Golden Eagle
Bald Eagle
Northern Harrier
Osprey
Prairie Falcon
Gyrfalcon
Merlin
American Kestrel
Blue Grouse
Spruce Grouse
Ruffed Grouse
White-Tailed Ptarmigan
Columbian Sharp-Tailed Grouse
Western Sage Grouse
Northern Bobwhite
California Quail

Mountain Quail
Chukar
Gray Partridge
Ring-Necked Pheasant
Turkey
Greater Sandhill Crane
Virginia Rail
Sora
Broad-Tailed Hummingbird
Rufous Hummingbird
Calliope Hummingbird
Belted Kingfisher
Common Flicker
Pileated Woodpecker
Lewis Woodpecker
Yellow-Bellied Sapsucker
Willianson's Sapsucker
Hairy Woodpecker
Downy Woodpecker
White-Headed Woodpecker
Blacked-Backed woodpecker
Eastern Kingbird
Western Kingbird
Ash-Throated Flycatcher
Say's Phoebe
Willow flycatcher
Hammond's Flycatcher
Dusky Flycatcher
Cordilleran flycatcher
Eastern Wood Peewee
Olive-Sided Flycatcher
Horned Lark
Violet Green Swallow
Tree Swallow
Northern Rough
    -Winged Swallow

Bank Swallow
Barn Swallow
Cliff Swallow
Gray Jay
Blue Jay
Stellar's Jay
Black-Billed Magpie
Common Raven
American Crow
Pinyon Jay
Clark's Nutcracker
Black-capped Chickadee
Mountain Chickadee
Chestnut-backed Chickadee
Bushtit
White-Breasted Nuthatch
Red-Breasted Nuthatch
Pygmy Nuthatch
Brown Creeper
Blue-Gray Gnatcatcher
Dipper
House Wren
Winter Wren
Marsh Wren
Canyon Wren
Rock Wren
Mockingbird
Gray Catbird
Sage Thrasher
American Robin
Varied Thrush
Veery
Swainson's Thrush
Hermit Thrush
Mountain Bluebird
Townsend's Solitaire

Golden-Crowned Kinglet
Ruby-Crown Kinglet
Water Pipit
Bohemian Waxwing
Cedar Waxwing
Northern Shrike
Loggerhead Shrike
Starling
Solitary Vireo
Red-Eyed Vireo
Warbling Vireo
Orange-Crowned Warbler
Nashville Warbler
Northern Parula
Yellow Warbler
Yellow-Rumped Warbler
Black-Throated Gray Warbler
Townsend's Warbler
Northern Waterthrush
MacGillvray's Warbler
American Restart
House sparrow
Lark Bunting
Bobolink
Western Meadowlark
Yellow-Headed Blackbird
Red-Winged Blackbird
Rusty Blackbird
Orchard Oriole
Brewer's Blackbird
Common Grackle
Brown-Headed Cowbird
Western Tanager
Rose-Breasted Grosbeak
Black-Head Grosbeak
Lazuli Bunting

Evening Grosbeak
Purple finch
Cassin's Finch
House Finch
Pine Grosbeak
Gray-Crowned Rosy Finch
Wallowa Rosy Finch
Black Rosy Finch
Pine Siskin
American Goldfinch
Redpoll
Lesser Goldfinch
Red Crossbill
White-Winged Cross Bill
Green-Tailed Towhee
Rufous-Sided Towhee
Savannah Sparrow
Bairds Sparrow
Grasshopper sparrow
Lark Sparrow
Sage Sparrow
Dark-Eyed Junco
Black-Chinned Sparrow
American Tree sparrow
Chipping Sparrow
Brewer's Sparrow
Harris Sparrow
White-Crowned Sparrow
Golden-Crowned Sparrow
Black-Throated Sparrow
Fox Sparrow
Lincoln's Sparrow
Song Sparrow
Lapland Longspur
Snow Bunting

MAMMALS

Montane Shrew
Vagrant Shrew
Dusky Shrew
Northern Water Shrew
Merriam Shrew
Pygmy Shrew
Coast Mole
Finged Myotis
Little Brown Myotis
Yuma Myotis
Long Eared Myotis
Long-Eared/
    Hairy Winged Myotis
California Myotis
Small-Footed Bat
Silvered-Haired Bat
Western Pipistrelle
Big Brown Bat
Hoary Bat
Spotted Bat
Townsend's Big-Eared Bat
Pallid Bat
Pika
Pygmy Rabbit
Mountain Cottontail
Snowshoe Hare
White-Tailed Jackrabbit
Black-Tailed Jackrabbit
Least Chipmunk
Yellow-Pine   chipmunk
Yellow-Bellied Marmot
Townsend's Ground Squirrel
Washington Ground Squirrel
Belding Ground Squirrel

Columbian Ground Squirrel
Northern Idaho
    Ground Squirrel
Mantled Ground Squirrel
Western Ground Squirrel
Eastern Ground Squirrel
Red Squirrel
Northern Flying Squirrel
Townsend's Pocket Gopher
Northern Pocket Gopher
Great Basin Pocket Mouse
Ord Kangaroo Rat
Beaver
Western Harvest Mouse
Canyon Mouse
Deer Mouse
Pinyon Mouse
Northern Grasshopper Mouse
Busy-Tailed Woodrat
Gapper Red-Backed Vole
Heather Vole
Long-Tailed Vole
Mountain Vole
Water Vole
Sagebrush Vole
Muskrat
Norway Rat
House Mouse
Western Jumping Mouse
Porcupine
Nutria
Coyote
Gray Fox
Red Fox
Black Bear
Raccoon

Pine Marten
Pacific Fisher
Short-Tailed Weasel
Long-Tailed Weasel
Mink
Wolverine
Badger
Spotted Skunk
Striped Skunk
River Otter
Puma
Feral House Cat
Bobcat
Feral Horse
Rocky Mountain Elk
Mule Deer
Idaho White-Tailed Deer
Moose
Pronghorn
Mountain Goat
California bighorn Sheep
Rocky Mountain Bighorn Sheep

INVERTEBRATES

Clams & Mussels
California Floater
Snails
Newcomb's Littorine Snail
Columbia Oregonian
Mission Creek Oregonian
Cottonwood Oregonian
Marbled Disc
River Limpet
Columbia Pebble Snail
Idaho Springsnail

Idaho Banded Mountain snail
Boulder Pile Mountain snail
Delicated
Mountain snail
Carinated Rocky
Whorled
Snake River Physa Snail
Hells Canyon Land Snail

Millipedes
Insects
Rockhoppers & Bristletails
Springtails
Mayflies
Dragonflies
Stonefilies
Cockroaches
Idaho Pointheaded
Grasshopper
Zoroterans
True Bugs
Hephill's Hydrobid
Black Nabicula Nabid

Cicdas & Allies
Lacewings 7 Allies

Beetles
Idaho Dunes Tiger Beetle
Columbia River Tiger Beetle
Blind Cave Beetle
Cantherid Beetle
Strawberry Mountain
    Gazelle Beetle
Labonte's Gazelle Beetle
Wallowa Snowfield

Carabid Beetle
Wallowa Mountains
Carabid Beetle

Scorpionflies & Allies
Flies
Butterflies
Western Meadow Fritillary
Silver-Bordered Fritillary
Dorothy's Acastus Checkerspot
Skinner's Sulpher
Colorado Hesperocimex
Hoary Elfin
Beartooth copper
Garita Skipper
Yuma Skipper

Barnes' Crescent
Peck's Skipper
Barnes' Crescent
Peck's Skipper
Long-Dash Skipper

Caddisflies
Blue Mountain Cryptochian

Ants, Bees & Wasps
Arachinids
Spiders
Pesudoscorpions
Harvestmen
Crustaceans
Fairy Shrimp

BIBLIOGRAPHY

Local Interest

Aitkenhead, Donna Ikenberry, *Eastern Oregon Wilderness Areas*, The Touchstone Press, 112 p., 1990.

Ashworth, William, *The Wallowas: Coming of Age in the Wilderness*, Oregon State University Press, Northwest Reprints Series, 192 p., 1998.

Bartlett, Grace, *From the Wallowas,* Pika Press, 144 p., 1992.

Barstad, Fred, *Hiking Oregon's Eagle Cap Wilderness*, Falcon Press, 312 p., 1996.

Bishop, Ellen Morris, and Allen, John Eliot, *Hiking Oregon's Geology*, The Mountaineers, 1996.

Brooks, Barbara and Thee, Karen, "Birds of Northeastern Oregon: Union, Baker, and Wallowa Counties", Grande Ronde Bird Club brochure, 1988.

Conley, Frank, and Wallowa Resource Council, *Hiking the High Wallowas and Hells Canyon*, Pika Press, revised edition, 80 p., 1995.

Douglas, William O., *Of Men and Mountains*, Harper and Brothers, New York, 338 p., 1950.

Douglas, William O., *My Wilderness; The Pacific West*, Doubleday and Company, New York, 206 p., 1960.

Hall, Troy and Shelby, Bo, "Eagle Cap Wilderness: Recreational Use and Impacts", a report submitted to the Eagle Cap Ranger District, Wallowa-Whitman National forest, February 8, 1994, Oregon State University.

Houle, Marcy, *The Prairie Keepers*, Addison-Wesley Publishing Co., 1995.

Josephy, Alvin M., *The Nez Perce Indians and the Opening of the Northwest*, University of Nebraska Press, 667 p., 1979.

Landers, Rich and Dolphin, Ida Rowe, *100 Hikes in the Inland Northwest*, The Mountaineers, 256 p., 1992.

Langston, Nancy, *Forest Dreams, Forest Nightmares*, University of Washington Press, 368 p., 1995.

Ostertag, Rhonda, and Ostertag, George, *50 Hikes in Hells Canyon and Oregon's Wallowas*, The Mountaineers, 1997.

Stevenson, Elmo, *Nature Rambles in the Wallowas*, reprint of 1937 publication, Pika Press, 110 p..

Vallier, Tracy, *Islands and Rapids: The Geologic Story of Hells Canyon*, *Confluence Press*, 168 p., 1998.

Wallowa Mountains, Eagle Cap Wilderness, Oregon, Topographic Map, Imus Geographics, Eugene, Oregon, 1995.

Wood, Wendell, *A Walking Guide to Oregon's Ancient Forests*, Oregon Natural Resources Council, 315 p., 1991.

Wuernther, George, *Oregon Mountain Ranges*, American Geographic Publishing, 104 p., 1987.

General Reading

Agee, James K., *Fire Ecology of Pacific Northwest Forests*, Island Press, 326 p., 1993.

Arno, Stephen F., and Hammerly, Ramona P., *Timberline; Mountain and Arctic Forest Frontiers*, The Mountaineers, 264 p., 1984.

Arno, Stephen F., and Gyer, Jane, *Discovering Sierra Trees*, Yosemite Natural History Association, 89 p., 1973.

Arno, Stephen F., and Hammerly, Ramona P., *Northwest Trees*, The Mountaineers, 222 p., 1977.

Bull, John, and Bull, Edith, *Birds of North America: Western Region*, Macmillan Field Guides, Collier Books, 144 p., 1989.

Foreman, Dave, and Wolke, Howie, *The Big Outside: A descriptive inventory of the big wilderness areas of the United States*. Harmony Books, 500 p., 1992.

Gabrielson, Ira N., and Jewett, Stanley G., *Birds of the Pacific Northwest; with special reference to Oregon*, Dover Publications, 650 p., 1970.

Kozloff, Eugene N., *Plants and Animals of the Pacific Northwest: An Illustrated Guide to the Natural History of Western Oregon, Washington, and British Columbia*, University of Washington Press, 264 p., 1982.

Kricher, John C., and Morrison, Gordon, *Ecology of Western Forests*, Peterson Field Guide Series, Houghton Mifflin Company, 554 p., 1993.

Little, Elbert L., *The Audubon Society Field Guide to North American Trees; Western Region*, Knopf Publishing Company, 640 p., 1989.

Maser, Chris, *Mammals of the Pacific Northwest*, Oregon State University Press, 416 p., 199.

Mathews, Daniel, *Cascade-Olympic Natural History: A Trailside Reference*, Raven Editions/Portland Audobon Society, 625 p., 1988.

McArthur, Lewis A., *Oregon Geographic Names*, Fifth Edition, Western Imprints, The Press of the Oregon Historical Society, 1982.

Oregon's Living Landscape: Strategies and Opportunities to Conserve Biodiversity, The Oregon Biodiversity Project, Defenders of Wildlife Publication, 218 p., 1998.

Orr, Elizabeth L., Orr, William N., and Baldwin, Ewart M., *Geology of Oregon*, Kendall/Hunt Publishing Company, 254 p., 1992.

Palmer, George, and Stuckey, Martha, *Western Tree Book: A Field Guide for Weekend Naturalists*, The Touchstone Press, 143 p., 1977.

Peattie, Donald C., *A Natural History of Western Trees*, Houghton Mifflin Company, 751 p., 1953.

Porsild, A.E., *Rocky Mountain Wildflowers*, National Museums of Canada, 454 p., 1979.

Ramsey, Fred L., *Birding Oregon*, Audubon Society of Corvallis, 134 p., 1978

Renner, Jeff, *Northwest Mountain Weather*, The Mountaineers, 112 p., 1992.

Ross, Charles R., *Trees to Know in Oregon*, Oregon State University Extension Service and Oregon State Forestry Department, 96 p., reprint 1991.

Rue, Leonard Lee, III, *Complete Guide to Game Animals: A Field Book of North American Species*, Outdoor Life Books/Van Nostrand Reinhold Company, 638 p., 1981.

Saling, Ann, *The Great Northwest Nature Factbook*, Alaska Northwest Books, 1991.

Schumann, Walter, *Handbook of Rocks, Minerals, and Gemstones*, Harper Collins Publishers and Houghton Mifflin Company, 380 p., 1993.

Strickler, Dee, *Wayside Wildflowers of the Pacific Northwest*, Falcon Press 272 p., 1993.

Sullivan, William L., *Exploring Oregon's Wild Areas*, The Mountaineers, 263 p., 1988.

Taylor, George H., and Hannan, Chris, *The Climate of Oregon: From Rain Forest to Desert*, Oregon State University Press, 224 p., 1999.

Taylor, George H., and Hatton, Raymond R., *The Oregon Weather Book: A State of Extremes*, Oregon State University Press, 288p., 1999.

Whitney, Stephen, *A Sierra Club Naturalists Guide to the Pacific Northwest*, Sierra Club Books, 342 p., 1989.

Whitney, Stephen, *Western Forests*, The Audobon Society Nature Guides, Alfred A. Knopf, 1985.

Zwinger, Ann H., and Willard, Beatrice E., *Land Above The Trees; A guide to American alpine tundra*, Harper and Row, 472 p., 1972.

Scientific Papers and Publications

Geology

Allen, John E., 1975, *"The Wallowa "Ice Cap" of Northeastern Oregon; An Exercise in the Interpretation of Glacial Landforms"*, The ORE BIN, Volume37, no. 12, Oregon Department of Geology and Mineral Industries.

Armstrong, Richard Lee, Taubeneck, William H., and Hales, Peter O., 1977, "Rb-Sr and K-Ar Geochronometry of Mesozoic Granitic Rocks and their Sr Isotopic Composition, Oregon, Washington, Idaho", *Geological Society of America Bulletin*, v. 88, p. 397-411.

Ave Lallement, H.G., Schmidt, W.J., and Kraft, J.L., 1985, "Major Late-Triassic Strike-Slip Displacement in the Seven Devils Terrane, Oregon and Idaho: A Result of Left-oblique Plate Convergence?", *Tectonophysics*, v. 119, p. 299-238.

Baksi, Ajoy K., 1989, "Reevaluation of the timing and duration of extrusion of the Imnaha, Picture Gorge, and Grande Ronde Basalts, Columbia River Basalt Group", p. 105-112, in Reidel, Stephen P and Hooper, Peter R., *Volcanism and Tectonism in the Columbia River Flood Basalt Province*, Geological Society of America Special Paper 239.

Blome, Charles D., and Nestell, Merylnd K., 1991, "Evolution of a Permo-Triassic Sedimentary Melange, Grindstone Terrane, east-central Oregon", *Geological Society of America Bulletin*, v. 103, p. 1280-1296.

Bonnichsen, B., 1985, "Dunite at New Meadows, Idaho- An Accreted Fragment of Oceanic Crust", *Geological Society of America Abstracts with Programs*, v. 17, 209.

Brandon, A.D., and Goles, G.G., 1988, "A Miocene Subcontinental Plume in the Pacific Northwest: Geochemical Evidence" *Earth and Planetary Science Letters* , v. 88, p. 273-283.

Burke, R.M., and Birkeland, P.W., 1983, "Holocene Glaciation in the Mountain Ranges of the Western United States", in *Late Quaternary Environments of the United States, Volume 2: The Holocene*, H.E. Wright, editor, University of Minnesota Press.

Carson, Robert J., "Which 25 km of coast, river, road, or trail in the USA has the greatest geologic diversity?", *Geological Society of America Abstracts with Programs*, 17:7, p. 540, 1985.

Carson, Robert J., "Stone pavements related to ice, with examples of alpine subnival boulder pavements from the Wallowa Mountains, Oregon, and the Beartooth Plateau, Montana", *Geological Society of America Abstracts with Programs*, v.125, A-158, 1993.

Carson, Robert J., in press, *Where the Rockies meet the Columbia Plateau: Geology from the Walla Walla Valley to the Wallowa Mountains, Oregon*, Keck Geology Symposium.

Carlson,.Richard W., and Hart, William K., 1988, "Flood Basalt Volcanism in the Northwestern United States", p. 35-62, in MacDougall,

192

J.D., *Continental Flood Basalts*, Klumer Academic Publishing, 342 p..

Catchings, R.D., and Mooney, W.D., 1988, "Crustal Structure of the Columbia Plateau: Evidence for Continental Rifting", *Journal of Geophysical Research*, p. 459-474.

Dickinson, William R., 1979, "Mesozoic Forearc Basin in central Oregon", *Geology*, v. 7, p. 1656-1700.

Geist, Dennis, and Richards, Mark, 1993, "Origin of the Columbia Plateau and Snake River plain: Deflection of the Yellowstone plume", *Geology*, v. 21, p. 789-792.

Hamilton, Warren B., 1963, "Metamorphism in the Riggins region, western Idaho", *United States Geological Survey Professional Paper* 436, 95 p..

Hamilton, Warren B., 1988, "Plate Tectonics and Island Arcs", *Geological Society of America Bulletin*, v. 100, p. 1503-1527.

Hillhouse, John W., Gromme, C. Sherman, and Vallier, Tracy L., 1982,"Paleomagnetism and Mesozoic Tectonics of the Seven Devils Volcanic Arc in Northeastern Oregon", *Journal of Geophysical Research*, v. 87, no. B5, p. 3777-3794.

Hooper, Peter R., and Conrey, R.M., 1989, "A Model for the Tectonic Setting of the Columbia River Basalt Eruptions", p. 293-306, in Reidel, Stephen P., and Hooper, Peter R., *Volcanism and Tectonism in the Columbia River Flood Basalt Province,* Geological Society of America Special Paper 239.

Hooper, Peter R., 1988, "The Columbia River Basalts", p. 1-34, in MacDougall, J.D., *Continental Flood Basalts*, Kluwer Academic Publishing,

342 p..

Manduca, Cathryn A., Kuntz, Mel A., and Silver, Leon T., 1993, "Emplacement and Deformation History of the western margin of the Idaho Batholith near McCall, Idaho; Influence of a Major Terrane Boundary", *Geological Society of America Bulletin*, v. 105, p. 749-765.

Mullen, Ellen D., 1985, "Petrologic Character of Permian and Triassic Greenstones from the Melange Terrane of eastern Oregon and their Implications for Terrane Origin", *Geology*, v. 13, p. 131-134.

Nelson, Dennis O., 1989, "Geochemistry of the Grande Ronde Basalt of the Columbia River Basalt Group; A Reevaluation of Source Control and Assimilation Effects", p. 333-342, in Reidel, Stephen P., and Hooper, Peter R., *Volcanism and Tectonism in the Columbia River Flood Basalt Province*, Geological Society of America Special Paper 239.

Pfaff, Virginia J., and Beeson, Marvin H., 1989, "Miocene basalt near Astoria, Oregon; Geophysical evidence for Columbia Plateau Origin", p.143-156, in Reidel, Stephen P., and Hooper, Peter R., *Volcanism and Tectonism in the Columbia River Flood Basalt Province*, Geological Society of America Special Paper 239.

Porter, Stephen C., Pierce, Kenenth L., and Hamilton, Thomas D., 1983, "Late Wisconsin Mountain Glaciation in the Western United States", in *Late Quaternary Environments of the United States, H.E. Wright, editor, Volume 1: The Late Pleistocene*, Stephen C. Porter, editor,University of Minnesota Press.

Reidel, Stephen P., 1989, "The Geologic Evolution of the central Columbia Plateau", p. 247-264, in Reidel, Stephen P., and Hooper, Peter

194

R., *Volcanism and Tectonism in the Columbia River Flood Basalt Province*, Geological Society of America Special Paper 239.

Reidel, Stephen P., Tolan, Terry L., Hooper, Peter R., Beeson, Marvin H., Fecht, Karl R., Bentley, Robert D., and Anderson, James Lee, 1989, "The Grande Ronde Basalt, Columbia River Basalt Group; Stratigraphic Descriptions and Correlations in Washington, Oregon, and Idaho", p. 21-54, in Reidel, Stephen P., and Hooper, Peter R., *Volcanism and Tectonism in the Columbia River Flood Basalt Province*, Geological Society of America Special Paper 239.

Sarewitz, Daniel, 1983, "Seven Devils: Is it really part of Wrengalia?", *Geology*, v. 11, p. 634-637.

Selverstone, Jane, Wernicke, Brian P., and Aliberti, Elaine A., 1992, "Intracontinental Subduction and Hinged Unroofing along the Salmon River Suture Zone, west-central Idaho", *Tectonics*, v. 11, p. 124-144.

Smith, Alan D., 1992, "Back-arc Convection Model for Columbia River Basalt Genesis", *Tectonophysics*, v. 207, p. 269-285.

Spencer, Patrick, Carson, Robert and Orr, William, "Pleistocene vertebrates and sediments near Wallowa Lake, Oregon." *Geological Society of America Abstracts with Programs*, 17:6, p.410, 1985.

Spencer, Patrick K., and Carson, Robert J., 1995, "The Enterprise Gravel: The Ancestral Wallowa River and Neotectonism in Northeastern Oregon", *Northwest Science*, Volume 69, Number 1, p. 60-71.

Strayer IV, Luther M., et al., 1989, "Direction and Shear Sense During Suturing of the Seven Devils-Wallowa Terrane against North America in western Idaho", *Geology*, v. 17, p. 1025-1028.

Stovall, J.C., "Pleistocene Geology and Physiography of the Wallowa Mountains (Oregon), with special reference to the Wallowa and Hurricane Canyons", M.S. Thesis, University of Oregon, Eugene, 1929.

Swanson, D.A., Cameron, K.A., Evants, R.C., Pringle, P.T., and Vance, J.A., "Cenozoic Volcanism in the Cascade Range and Columbia Plateau, southern Washington and northern Oregon", pp.16-20, in Chapin, Charles E., and Zidek, Jiri, *Field Excursions to Volcanic terranes in the Western United States, Volume II, Cascades and Intermountain West*, New Mexico Bureau of Mines and Mineral Resources, Memoir 47, 286 p., 1989.

Tolan, Terry L., Reidel, Stephen P., Beeson, Marvin H., Anderson, James Lee, Fecht, Karl R., and Swanson, Donald A., 1989, "Revisions to the estimates of the areal extent and volume of the Columbia River basalt group", p.1-19, in Reidel, Stephen P and Hooper, Peter R., *Volcanism and Tectonism in the Columbia River Flood Basalt Province*, Geological Society of America Special Paper 239.

Vallier, Tracy, and Brooks, Howard C., 1986, Geologic Implications of Paleozoic and Mesozoic Paleontology and Biostratigraphy, Blue Mountains Province, Oregon and Idaho, USGS Professional Paper 1435, Part 1 of a series, *Geology of the Blue Mountains Region of Oregon, Idaho, and Washington*, United States Geological Survey, 93p..

Vallier, Tracy, and Brooks, Howard C., 1987, The Idaho Batholith and Its Border Zone, USGS Professional Paper 1436, Part 2 of a series, *Geology of the Blue Mountains Region of Oregon, Idaho, and Washington*, United States Geological Survey, 196p..

Vallier, Tracy, and Brooks, Howard C.,1990, Cenozoic Geology of the Blue Mountains Region, USGS Professional Paper 1437, Part 3 of a series, *Geology of the Blue Mountains Region of Oregon, Idaho, and Washington*, United States Geological Survey, 135p..

Vallier, Tracy, and Brooks, Howard C.,1995, Petrology and Tectonic Evolution of Pre-Tertiary Rocks of the Blue Mountains Region, USGS Professional Paper 1438, Part 4 of a series, *Geology of the Blue Mountains Region of Oregon, Idaho, and Washington*, United States Geological Survey, 539p..

Vallier, Tracy, and Brooks, Howard C.,1994, Stratigraphy, Physiography, and Mineral Resources of the Blue Mountains Region, USGS Professional Paper 1439, Part 5 of a series, *Geology of the Blue Mountains Region of Oregon, Idaho, and Washington*, United States Geological Survey, 198p..

Weis, Paul L., Gualtieri, J.L., Cannon, William F., and Tucher, Ernest T., McMahan, Arel B., Federspiel, Francis E., *Mineral Resources of the Eagle Cap Wilderness and Adjacent Areas, Oregon*, United States Geological Survey Open File Report, 1972.

White, James D.L., White, David L., Vallier, Tracy, Stanley Jr., George D., and Ash, Sidney R., 1992, "Middle Jurassic Strata Link Wallowa, Olds Ferry, and Izee Terranes in the Accreted Blue Mountain Island Arc, northeastern Oregon", *Geology*, v. 20, p. 729-732.

Williams, Larry D., "Neoglacial Landforms and Neoglacial Chronology of the Wallowa Mountains, Northeastern Oregon", M.S. Thesis, University of Massachusetts, Amherst, 1974.

Wilson, Douglas, and Cox, Allan, 1980, "Paleomagnetic Evidence for Tectonic Rotation of Jurassic Plutons in Blue Mountains, Eastern Oregon",

Journal of Geophysical Research, v. 85, no. B7, p. 3681-3689.

Flora

Burns, Russell M., and Honkala, Barbara H., 1990, Silvics of North America; Volume 1. Conifers, USDA Forest Service Agricultural Handbook 654, 675 p..

Carlson, Clinton E., Byler, James W., and Dewey, Jerald E., 1995, "Western Larch: Pest-Tolerant Conifer of the Northern Rocky Mountains," in Schmidt, Wyman C., and McDonald, Kathy J., Ecology and Management of Larix Forests: A Look Ahead, Proceedings of an International Symposium, Whitefish, MT., 1992, USDA Forest Service, General Technical Report, GTR-INT-319, Intermountain Research Station.

Cole, David N., 1982, "Vegetation of Two Drainages in the Eagle Cap Wilderness, Wallowa Mountains, Oregon." USDA Forest Service, Research Paper INT-288, Intermountain Forest and Range Experiment Station, Ogden, UT.

Daubenmire, R., 1966,"Vegetation: Identification of typal communities." Science, v.151, p. 291-298.

Debyle, Norbert V., and Winokur, Robert P., 1985, Aspen: Ecology and Management in the Western United States, USDA Forest Service General Technical Report RM-119.

Evenden, Angela G., 1995, "Larix Lyalli and Larix Occidentalis Within USDA Forest Service Research Natural Areas," in Schmidt, Wyman C., and McDonald, Kathy J., Ecology and Management of Larix Forests: A Look Ahead, Proceedings of an International Symposium, Whitefish, MT. 1992, USDA Forest Service, General Technical Report GTR-INT-319, Intermountain Research Station.

Fiedler, Carl E., and Lloyd, Dennis A., 1995, "Autecology and Synecology of Western Larch," in Schmidt, Wyman C., and McDonald, Kathy J., *Ecology and Management of Larix Forests: A Look Ahead, Proceedings of an International Symposium*, Whitefish, MT., 1992, USDA Forest Service, General Technical Report GTR-INT-319, Intermountain Research Station.

Franklin, Jerry F., and Dyrness, C.T., 1973, *Natural Vegetation of Oregon and Washington*, PNW Forest and Range Experiment Station, USDA Forest Service General Technical Report PNW-8, 417 p..

Hall, Frederick C., 1973, "Plant Communities of the Blue Mountains in Eastern Oregon and Southeastern Washington." USDA Forest Service, Pacific Northwest Region, R6 Area Guide 3-1, 62 p.

Hall, Frederick C., 1974, "Key to Environmental Indicator Plants of the BlueMountains in Eastern Oregon and Southeastern Washington" USDA Forest Service, Pacific Northwest Region, R6 Area Guide 3-2, 51 p.

Head, Serge Conrad, 1959, "Plant Taxonomy and Ecology of the East Eagle Creek Drainage of the Wallowa Mountains, Northeastern Oregon." Ph.D. Thesis, Oregon State College,.

Jaindl, Raymond G., and Quigley, Thomas M., editors, 1992, *Search for a Solution:Sustaining the Land, People, and Economy of the Blue Mountains*, American Forests.

Johnson, Charles G. Jr., and Simon, Steven A., 1987, *Plant Associations of the Wallowa-Snake Province,* United States Forest Service Publication R-6 ECOL-TP-225A-86,.

Johnson, Charles G. Jr., 1996, "Blue and Wallowa Mountains Grasslands: Integral Components of the Landscape", *Sustaining Rangeland Ecosystems, Proceedings of a Symposium,* EOSC, La Grande, 1994, OSU Extension Service, Special Report 953.

Johnson, Charles G., Jr., 1994, "Forest Health in the Blue Mountains: A Plant Ecologist's Perspective on Ecosystem Processes and Biological Diversity", USDA Forest Service General Technical Report PNW-GTR-339.

Johnson, Charles G., Jr., Clausnitzer, Roderick R., Mehringer, Peter J., and Oliver, Chadwick D., 1994, "Biotic and Abiotic Processes of Eastside Ecosytems: The Effects of Management on Plant and Community Ecology, and on Stand and Landscape Vegetation Dynamics", USDA Forest Service, Pacific Northwest Research Station, General Technical Report PNW-GTR-322.

Johnson, Charles G., Jr., *Common Plants of the Inland Pacific Northwest,* USDA Forest Service Pacific Northwest Region, R6-ERW-TP051-93.

Lehmkul, J.F., Hessburg, P.F., Everett, R.L., Huff, M.H., and Ottman, R.D., 1994, "Historical and current forest landscapes of Eastern Oregon and Washington. Part 1:Vegetation patterns and insect and disease hazards," USDA Forest Service, Pacific Northwest Research Station, General Technical Report PNW-GTR-328.

Mason, Georgia, 1975, *Guide to the Plants of the Wallowa Mountains of Northeastern Oregon,* Museum of Natural History, University of Oregon, 411p.

Reid, Elbert H., Strickler, Gerald S., and Hall, Wade B., 1980, "Green Fescue Grassland: 40 Years of Secondary Succession", USDA Forest Service, Pacific Northwest Forest and Range Experiment Station, Research Paper PNW-274, 39p..

Scharpf, Robert F., 1993, *Diseases of Pacific Coast Conifers*, USDA Forest Service, Agricultural Handbook 521, 199p..

Schmidt, Wyman C., and Shearer, Raymond C., 1995, "Larix Occidentalis ; a Pioneer of the North American West," in Schmidt, Wyman C., and McDonald, Kathy J., *Ecology and Management of Larix Forests: A Look Ahead, Proceedings of an International Symposium*, Whitefish, MT., 1992, USDA Forest Service, General Technical Report GTR-INT-319, Intermountain Research Station.

Skovllin, J.M., Harris, R.W., Strickler, G.S., and Garrison, G., 1976," Effects of cattle-grazing methods on ponderosa pine-bunchgrass range in the Pacific Northwest." USDA Forest Service Technical Bulletin 1531, 324.

Strickler, Gerald S., and Hall, Wade B., 1980, "The Standley Allotment: A History of Range Recovery," USDA Forest Service, Pacific Northwest Forest and Range Experiment Station, Research Paper PNW-278, 35 p..

Sudworth, George B., 1967, *Forest Trees of the Pacific Slope*, Dover Publications, republication of 1908 edition, 455 p..

Walstad, John D., Radovesich, Steven R., and Sandberg, David V., 1990, *Natural and Prescribed Fire in Pacific Northwest Forests*, Oregon State University Press.

Wissmar, R.C., Smith, J.E., McIntosh, B.A., Li, H.W., Reeves, G.H., and Sedell, J.R., 1994, "Ecological Health of river basins in forested regions of eastern Washington and Oregon." USDA Forest Service Pacific Northwest Research Station, General Technical report PNW-GTR-326.

Woodland, Dennis W., 1965, "A Vegetational Study of Unit and Razz Lakes in the Wallowa Mountains, Northeastern Oregon." M.A. Thesis, Walla Walla College.

Zika, Peter F., and Alverson, Edward R., "Ferns new to the Wallowa Mountains, Oregon", *American Fern Journal*, v. 86, 2, p. 61-64, 1996.

Fauna

Csuti, B., Kimmerling, A.J., O'Neil, T.A., Shaughnesy, M.M., Gaines, E.P., and Huso, M.M.P., 1997, *Atlas of Oregon Wildlife: Distribution, habitat, and natural history.* Oregon State University Press,

Dobkin, D.S., 1995, Management and conservation of sage grouse, denominative species for the ecological health of shrub steppe ecosystems. USDI Bureau of Land Management.

Johnsgard, Paul A., 1986, *Birds of the Rocky Mountains*, University of Nebraska Press, 504 p..

Marshall, David B., 1996, *Species at Risk: Sensitive, Threatened and Endangered Vertebrates of Oregon*, Oregon Department of Fish and Wildlife, second edition.

Matthews, Patrick E., and Coggins, Vic L., 1994, "Status and History of mountain goats in Oregon," Biennial Symposium Northern Wild Sheep and Goat Council.

McIntosh, B.A., Sedell, J.R., Smith, J.E., Wissmar, R.C., Clarke, S.E., Reeves, G.H., and Brown, L.A., 1994. " Management history of east-side ecosystems: Changes in fish habitat over 50 years, 1935-1992." USDA Forest Service, Pacific Northwest Research Station, General Technical Report PNW-GTR- 327.

Nehls, Harry, *Familiar Birds of the Northwest: covering birds commonly found in Oregon, Washington, Idaho, northern California, and western Canada,* Portland Audobon Society, 1989.

Raynes, Bert, 1984. *Birds of Grand Teton National Park,* Grand Teton Natural History Association, 90 p..

Sturges, Franklin Wright, 1957, "Habitat Distributions of Birds and Mammals in Lostine Canyon, Wallowa Mountains, Northeast Oregon." Ph.D. Thesis, Oregon State College.

Verts, B.J., and Carraway, Leslie N., *Keys to the Mammals of Oregon,* Oregon State University, 178 p.

Wildlife Habitats in Managed Forests, the Blue Mountains of Oregon and Washington, 1979, USDA Forest Service Agricultural Handbook no. 553.

Wauer, Roland, 1993, *The Visitor's Guide to the Birds of the Rocky Mountain NationalParks; United States and Canada,* John Muir Publications, 422 p.

INDEX

Page numbers listed first, then figure numbers in *italics*, then plate numbers in **bold**.